Keep
It
Simple &
Sane

Keep It Simple & Sane

Freeing Yourself
from Addictive Thinking

Barb Rogers

Conari Press

First published in 2008 by Conari Press,
an imprint of Red Wheel/Weiser, LLC

With offices at:
500 Third Street, Suite 230
San Francisco, CA 94107
www.redwheelweiser.com

ISBN: 978-1-57324-357-5

LIBRARY OF CONGRESS CATALOGING-IN-PUBLICATION DATA
available upon request.

Cover and text design by Maxine Ressler
Typeset in Bembo Std and Impressum

Printed in Canada
TCP
10 9 8 7 6 5 4 3 2 1

Dedication

To my friends, Don & Carol McQuinn.
You mean so much to me.
Thank you for your love and support.

To Tom, my husband, and the love of my life.
I would marry you all over again.

And, to the memory of Josh Rodgers
and Nick Tibbetts, who we lost this past year.
You will both be missed.

Contents

Acknowledgments

A special thank-you to my friends and family members at a distance, who stay in touch even though I can't email. Your cards, letters, and calls mean so much.

Tammi Clancy, Tom & Jacqui McKibben, David & Susie Tibbetts, Karla Backlund, Elva Adams, Chassie West, Joan Highland, Laura Pasten, Jennifer Martin, Flemming & Julia Pedersen, Dottie Ashton, Ken Fox & Ken Epperly, Jim & Wanda LaBounty, Ruth Belden, Arnold & Phoebe Bitner, Cheryl Robinson, Roxy Gantes, Marie Reid, Elaine Flinn, Maree Gutterson, Gala Kimberline, Roslyn Hartman, Susan Miller, Joyce Hammock, Chris Brown, Don & Phil Rodgers.

And, to my snowbird friends, Susie & Pat Haag, and the Sunday morning gratitude group, my love and thanks.

Introduction

The past is history, the future is a mystery. All you must truly be concerned with is the present. No matter what has gone before, you have the option to make changes, to make new choices, right now. No matter what you think the future might hold, to live in hope or dread of things yet to come robs you of this moment in time. It is a moment you will never get back. If you let it pass by unnoticed, unexplored, whose fault is that? What if it was one of those pivotal moments that might have altered your journey in life?

The truth is, life is simple. You're born, you live however long, and you die. As a human being, you need air, water, food, and shelter to survive. It doesn't matter if you live in a mansion, drink from a gold tap, and eat food prepared by a chef, or live in a box, drink from a hose, and eat from a trash can. Our basic needs are what we have in common.

It is people that are complicated. It is the "wants" that separate us from one another. The conflict between the reality that is your life and the perception of what you believe it should be is the beginning of the complications.

There are those who blame progress. They say, "Life used to be simpler." Perhaps that's because there weren't as many options and choices in the past. Those very options and choices that may be to blame for complicating life are the answer to living an uncluttered, simpler life.

Progress is responsible for new medications and surgeries that make it possible to live a healthier, longer life. On the other hand, drugs have drawn some into addiction and misery. Was it the drug, or the choice to abuse it, or use it for another purpose, that was to blame? Through new inventions, life has become easier, allowing more time for other activities. I've heard others make the comment, "He (or she) has too much time on his (or her) hands," as if that explained why the person got into trouble. Extra time is not the problem. A lack of appreciation and poor choices of what to do with extra time is the problem.

Do you imagine a young person in the 1700s, who had to chop wood for heat and cooking, draw water from a well for drinking and bathing, and plow fields with a horse-drawn plow, didn't get in trouble? Sure, the individual may have had less time, been more exhausted, but it is about choices.

Throughout life there are pivotal moments when the choice you make will alter your life path. Consider the pivotal moments in your life, the choices you've made—unless you suffer from a mental illness that renders you incapable of making a rational decision, you *chose* the life you have. You consciously set your feet upon the path that you have followed. Your life, your happiness or misery, your attitudes, fears, and outlook on life, are your responsibility.

I understand how difficult it is to stay in the present and to take responsibility. For many, too many, years, the past didn't have a hold on me—I had a hold on it. It was a handy excuse to justify my inappropriate behavior, my attitude, and it was always there when I needed to pull it out and use it. I used the future for procrastination and castles built on air. I'll do it tomorrow. Things will be better next week, next month, or next year. Someday my prince will come along and rescue me from my life.

The truth was that no one could rescue me from my life, except me. They could love me, care for me, do for me what I could not do for myself, even support me financially, but that wouldn't solve my problem. My life was not what I wanted it to be because I was not who I wanted to be. Something was broken within, and no one, or nothing, could fix it but me. It was an inside job, and until I became willing to go on that inside journey, nothing would change.

I'd heard the catchphrase "keep it simple" used by therapists, doctors, and recovery programs, and I'd always thought it was just something cute to put on a plaque or hang on the wall. But I began to wonder, how does one do that? How does one "keep it simple"? And could it really help? I'd always told myself life is complicated, and continued to live in chaos, constantly overwhelmed. Maybe there was something to this beyond a slogan.

It wasn't until I grabbed onto the "keep it simple" concept that I understood about taking life—with all its ups and downs and events out of our control—down to small bites and living in the moment that I found relief.

If you're sincerely interested in simplifying your life, releasing yourself from the clutter that holds you back, there are four facets to consider: mental clutter, emotional clutter, spiritual clutter, and physical clutter. Emotions and thoughts cluttered by past experiences and old feelings, elusive dreams of the future, and a spirituality that creates in you a core conflict between beliefs and actions will all manifest in your physical life. In order to simplify, to unclutter, to live the life you desire, it will be necessary to explore each of the four facets.

If you anticipate the journey's end, my guess is you will sell yourself short. If you take time to savor the moments and enjoy the process, you will be amazed at all the treasures you will amass along the way. The end of this particular journey won't come until your days are done. Will you be satisfied with the moments of your life, the choices you made?

Keep
It
Mentally
Simple

A ring of the bell,
A knock at the door,
and life can change forever.
—Anonymous

What Were You Thinking?

We are the great thinkers of the world. By that, I don't mean that what we think is necessarily great, but that we think a great deal of the time. No matter what we are doing, the mind continues to ponder, imagine, ruminate, cogitate, consider, and contemplate. It is one busy little organ. Where do all these thoughts come from?

As far as anyone knows for certain, you enter this world with a clean slate. However, more recently, I understand there are people experimenting with influencing the mind of a baby while it's still in the womb. They talk to the fetus, play specific music, even try to teach it . . . as if this little person isn't going to have enough to think about once he or she gets here! I wonder if these people consider the fact that if the fetus can hear and learn, then it is hearing and learning *all* the time, not just when the researcher is speaking to it. There I go thinking again.

When we first start out, how we think and what we think about the world, ourselves, and others, is formed by those who are significant in our lives. They bring with them what they were taught, their life experiences, and their specific beliefs. To fit into the community of family, we tend to accept these truths as fact. Why wouldn't we believe them, even when they tell us negative things about ourselves, others, the world around us? These are the people who are supposed to love us, protect us, nurture us, and prepare us for life as adults.

School begins, and we enter a community of peers, teachers, and discover that not everyone thinks like we do, like our family. It can be a time when confusion, frustration, and conflict begin.

Having spent a great deal of my pre-school years as a river rat, barefoot and free, frolicking in the sunshine, splashing in the cold water of central Illinois's Kaskaskia River, playing on the old covered bridge, it was devastating when I began school. I was not prepared. There were rules, so many rules, and so many strangers. It was the early 1950s, and girls were required to wear dresses and act ladylike. I had no idea what that meant. However, they stuffed me into a secondhand dress, white socks, and shoes. Accustomed to bib overalls, shorts, and pants, I ended up tearing every one of the high-waisted dresses at the waist by continually pulling on them. My white socks were always black because I took my shoes off every chance I got. I was more comfortable with boys because they didn't mind exploring, defying, or getting dirty.

By the time I entered the third grade, I believed I was a poor, black child. I didn't know we were poor until we lived in town, on the wrong side of the tracks. If I hadn't been so dark-complected, if my mother hadn't attempted a home permanent that turned into an afro, if we hadn't lived in an all-black neighborhood, I could have been white trash. Back then, that was a step up. But no, I joined my ethnic community. The problem was, I didn't belong to the African American community, and they let me know it. I was a girl, but I didn't think like other girls. I was white, but I didn't look white. The conflict between what I thought and the reality that was my life grew.

As important as it is to find your place in your family, it is just as important to have a sense of belonging to your peer community and your ethnic community. When you don't have that, you begin to think something is wrong with you, that you are not worthy. From that point on, life becomes very complicated.

At some point we got a television. That was a big deal in the 1950s. Little did I know the impact it would have on my life. I sat mesmerized by the small black-and-white shows and the commercials. Fascinated by the products and ideas on the commercials, I began to think. Who got to have those things? Why weren't we like the families at the table eating a special breakfast cereal together? Television families didn't treat their kids like I was treated. They taught them lessons in a nice way. There was no screaming, no hitting, no being shunned or locked away. They didn't tell them they were lazy, stupid, or ugly, that if they had a brain they would take it out and play with it.

My mind told me that if we could just return to the river, to the simplicity of our lives, away from strangers with their different ideas, away from televisions, electricity, running water, flush toilets, I could stop worrying, stop thinking, stop trying to be something or someone that I wasn't. It was my earliest real thought of escape.

I simply wanted to put on my baggy bibs, feel the sun on my face, the sand between my toes, and watch the river flow. I wanted to go back to that place where I knew I was safe, where I no longer had to think about how I looked, how I acted, what I should be learning, and where I didn't have to care about what we had and didn't have compared to others.

I blamed my parents. It wasn't my idea to change our life. I didn't have a choice. They dragged me along with them, and my misery was all their fault. I would never forgive them.

It's amazing how you can hold on to a thought or idea for years, and let it continue to affect your life, keeping you from the very things you thought you desired most. If the thought or idea stays in your brain long enough, it begins to atrophy, becoming a degenerative disease that keeps you sick.

By age 10, the seeds of my degenerative disease of the mind were planted. I thought all the time, and all I thought about was myself. What was I thinking? That because I was poor, I would never have those things that made other people happy. That because my parents didn't seem to like me,

I was unworthy of love. That because of how I looked, I would never fit in with others. That because I was stupid, I would never succeed. Any attention I hoped to get would be because I did something bad.

The only hope I had was to escape. The problem was that no matter how far I went, where I ended up, or who I was with, I took my diseased mind right along with me into every situation, and every relationship. Each time I failed, every time I gave in to fear of trying, when I did bad things to get the attention I craved so badly, I nurtured the seeds and allowed them to take root.

Like the old, dirty, dusty clutter that can accumulate in a house, the stuff you don't need but are afraid to get rid of in case you might need it someday, those old thoughts can pile up. Why do we keep them? The only use they have is an excuse not to be responsible, not to move forward, not to risk facing the unknown. When fear strikes, it's comforting to know that we can go wallow in that old stuff, surround ourselves with memories, even bad ones, and justify our fear. After all, if we can hold on to the past, those old ideas, we can't be blamed for anything we've done, or are going to do. We can become the great thinking martyr.

What were you thinking about yourself, others, the world around you, at age 10? How about age 16 . . . 20 . . . 25? What old thoughts are you holding on to? Do you suffer from the mind clutter disease? It is a symptomatic disease that shows itself through poor self-esteem, irrational insecurities and fears, and low self-worth. Untreated, the results of the disease may be a discontented, frustrated, unhappy human being, who is stuck in outdated, unhealthy ideas.

The brain is a miraculous organ when it is not clogged up. However, like every other amazing machine, when there is a problem, you must identify it, figure out a way to fix it so it doesn't reoccur, and then remedy the problem. The next step is to keep it running by consistent use . . . never letting it get clogged up again.

I was well into my thirties when I stopped numbing my brain with mind-altering substances to escape my thoughts, and decided there had to be a better way to live, to think, to function. It was time to delve into those nooks and crannies of my mind, to discover what was there, and to clean out the old, useless rubbish from my past. It had been piling up for a long time. Some of it was really stuck. It would take some time and effort to accomplish a clean sweep.

It can take anything from self-examination to therapy to arrest the disease, depending on how far along it is and how embedded the old thoughts are in your mind. Before you run off and pay thousands of dollars for extensive therapy, there are some simple exercises you can try yourself that may work for you.

Imagine yourself as an explorer. What you will be exploring throughout this book are the caves in your brain. You will be shining a light on all those dark corners to see what you can discover. Those old ideas can only affect you as long

Don't "Should" on Yourself

Images! They are everywhere. If you enjoy browsing magazines and catalogues, watching television, listening to the radio, and scanning the Internet, you know what I mean. Even a Sunday drive is filled with signs and billboards. Every day, in every way, you are shown what you "should" look like, what you "should" strive to obtain, what you "should" think and believe, how you "should" act, to be a successful member of society.

The use of images in this way is called, "social engineering," which is essentially calculating a scheme and manipulating or directing an enterprise through skillful or artful contrivance. That's quite a mouthful. Put simply, it means to take a person, product, or idea, and figure out a way to make it acceptable, even desirable, to as many people as possible.

You might be wondering why social engineering is something for concern. How does it affect you? The effect may be greater than you think. People want to fit in with the society in which they are living. What happens if they don't believe they are a part of it all, or are treated like they are not?

The fallout can be as simple as an unhappy, unfulfilled life, or so severe that it results in mental illness, crime, suicide, addictions, and other obsessive behavior. If you think

I exaggerate, perhaps you haven't shared my experiences. Allow me to take you along, not only on my personal journey, but into the hospitals, jails and prisons, and treatment facilities that are filled to overflowing with those who figured out what life "should" be, but couldn't figure out how to accomplish it.

One definition of a victim in *Merriam-Webster's Collegiate Dictionary* is "one that is acted on and usually adversely affected by a force or agent." I began life as a victim. I was a victim of poverty, of angry parents in an unhappy alliance that resulted in neglect and abuse, of not believing I had any worth. When I got to school, the idea that I was not worthy was further pounded home by other children, even teachers, through thoughtless words and actions. I did not belong . . . not at home, not at school, not anywhere.

Before I hit puberty, I'd figured some things out in my little victimized brain. I would never look the way I "should," the way others looked. I didn't think like others. My life was not like my peers, not like the families I saw on television, in magazines. The only power I had, the only time I felt an inkling of love, was through sex. Power came because I was the great keeper of secrets. Because I was such a victim, feeling powerless most of the time, I grabbed on to anything, many times bad things, that made me feel like I had some control.

If you think sex is not a powerful tool, pay attention to the movies and commercials on television for one day. I'm amazed at the number and variety of products, from mustard to brakes, that are still sold by using sex. Apparently sex sells or advertisers wouldn't be using it.

I didn't like sex, but it was the tool I could use to get my needs, no matter how skewed, met. As I've worked with others over the years who have also prostituted themselves, I hear the same story. They used sex for power, and substituted it for love. For most of them, including myself, love is either not real or too frightening to consider. To truly care about another human being is to lose power and invite pain.

As if you think I couldn't sink any lower, because I hated what I believed I had to do, I sought mind-numbing substances. There was a time when I would put anything in my mouth that would shut out the truth. Thank God I was afraid of needles, or you would have found me in some alley shooting up.

I had a baby before I had a driver's license. It seems odd now. I didn't know how to drive a car, but I thought I could mother a child. Talk about not thinking right. But for the first time in my life, when I looked into the face of my child, I knew love. Babies don't know any better. They love unconditionally. Tears are welling in my eyes just thinking about the day I gave birth, that moment, and what was to follow.

Addicts in recovery will tell you that it was that first high that got them hooked, and that they spent years trying to recapture that feeling. For me, and many others, having a baby was just like that. I told myself it was okay to keep having babies because that's what women "should" do, but really I was chasing the feeling.

My poor babies failed to thrive and died in infancy, except for my eldest son, who would live to be my caretaker until his early death at age 15. What a horrible burden to put on such small shoulders.

Living in Your Head Can Be Dangerous

The older I got, the more "shoulds" there were. I failed at all of them. The conflict between what I "should" be and all the failures drove me to a mental hospital. I was 25 years old and had lost my mind. After my release, clean of alcohol and drugs, except the ones prescribed by a psychiatrist, I spent years in therapy. I was shocked, drugged, analyzed, hypnotized, and later educated.

It was when I chose to go off the prescription drugs that the crap hit the fan and blew right back into my face. I "should" have been a better person, daughter, wife, mother, friend, employee, even patient. My mind would scream, "I want to . . . I want to be part of you, to understand how I'm supposed to live, to think, to be . . . I want to, but I don't know how." It was time to face the mirror, and it wasn't a pretty picture. How in the world would I ever resolve my past, forgive myself, and learn to live the way I "should"?

Living from the neck up, in avoidance of feelings, is an old trick victims use for survival. Because I couldn't stand the truth, the memories, my thoughts, I returned to mind-numbing substances—and not the ones prescribed by a doctor. Although, if they were handy, I'd take them, too, whether they were prescribed for me or someone else. Believe me when I tell you, you wouldn't have wanted me near your medicine cabinet.

I knew, on some level, that if I ever allowed my emotions to invade my mind, they would overwhelm me, and I would lose my mind again. I lived on the edge of insanity for years.

So often, when I work with addicts or victims of abuse, I tell them they have to stop living in their head. It's a dangerous place to be. Thoughts are like a pressure valve. If pushed down and held in long enough, eventually they will explode in unhealthy ways. This reminds me of a man I've known for many years, both during the time we were using and when we got clean and sober. A victim of childhood abuse, who became a raging alcoholic and drug addict, in and out of this institution and that, he finally sought help.

He has been clean and sober for many years now, but he still lives in his head, afraid that if he ever reveals his secrets, his feelings, it will kill him. For years he's tried to be what a person in recovery "should" be. However, there is conflict between his thoughts and his actions. Even though, as far as

I know, he has never used again, his life is one disaster after another.

He has pushed away everyone who cares for him, is not able to have a long-lasting relationship, or even friendship, and others avoid him at every opportunity. There is a hurt, frustrated, angry little boy living in his mind, in charge of his grown-up body. If he continues to live like this, who only knows what will happen. One thing I do know is that it won't be good.

An obsession of the mind can be as destructive as a cancer eating away at your body. It will clutter up every dream you have, every goal you've set for yourself, every relationship you've wished for, and any hope for peace and happiness.

He Planted a Seed in My Mind

How do you stop being a victim of your mind? One of the first things you can do is omit the word "should" from your mind and your vocabulary. When you think, "I should have done it differently" or "I should be able to do it better," stop!

Did you catch that? I said *stop*.

If you could have done it differently, you would have. You were exactly where you were at the moment, working with whatever you had to work with, and you could not be any more, or any less, than you were. When you discover the truth of this, and accept it, you will come to understand that it is also true for others. If you embrace the idea that we do the best we can with what we have, you will discover the path to an uncluttered mind.

"As long as you hold on to pain, you will cause others pain," a young man in prison told me. He was born to a family of alcoholics and drug addicts and experienced every form of abuse. When under the influence, he became an abuser, eventually ending up in prison for murdering a friend. With tears in his eyes, he said, "I didn't want to be like them, but I didn't know any other way to be."

I asked him what changed. I thought perhaps it was getting caught and the prospect of spending the greater part of his life behind bars, so I was surprised at his answer. "I had to forgive them," he said, "and then forgive myself."

I knew some of the details of his story. Still in early recovery from my own addictions, still blaming others from my past for my problems, I could not imagine how he could forgive what was done to him. I looked into his young, sincere face. He meant it. When I left him, his words, those deep brown eyes reflecting a peace of mind I had yet to experience, haunted me. Was the answer to clearing out the clutter of my mind and the pain that lived on in every thought simply forgiveness?

He had planted a seed in my mind. The seed took root and grew as I explored the idea of forgiveness. I spent more time with this young man, and others like him, and listened to their stories, their solutions. They were in prison, I was on the outside, but I couldn't have been more locked up if I'd been in a cage. My prison bars were formed by painful thoughts from the past, fear of letting go of the pain because I wouldn't have an excuse left. According to them, the key to open my prison was forgiveness.

It's relatively easy to say, "I forgive you," but an entirely different thing to mean it. If it's not real, it won't work.

But how? A young friend once asked me if I'd ever read the Prayer of St. Francis. I informed him I wasn't religious. He said it didn't matter, that I should read it anyway. I wasn't thrilled about the idea of a prayer, but curiosity got the better of me. I located it. It reads:

PRAYER OF ST. FRANCIS

Lord, make me an instrument of Your peace.
Where there is hatred, let me sow love;
where there is injury, pardon;
where there is doubt, faith;
where there is despair, hope;
where there is darkness, light;
and where there is sadness, joy.
O, Divine Master,
grant that I may not so much seek
to be consoled as to console;
to be understood, as to understand;
to be loved as to love;
for it is in giving that we receive;
it is in pardoning that we are pardoned;
and it is in dying that we are given eternal life.

Every time I read the prayer, one word jumped out at me: "pardon." Yes, search as I might, I kept returning to this idea of forgiveness.

The next to the last line told me that the only way I would be able to forgive myself was first to find a way to forgive others, to forgive what was done to me. To stop holding anger and resentment toward those who had hurt me. The way to forgiveness is through understanding. You want to be understood, for others to have compassion for your self-imposed prison. You can do this. Through total forgiveness, you can be the person you want to be. Change those things about yourself that are holding you back, not because you should, but because it's what you want.

If you are thinking you can't do it, that there's simply no way you can forgive those who hurt you, or yourself for hurting others, you need to understand that from this moment on, you are no longer a victim, but a volunteer.

Flower Power

You try to eat a balanced diet to stay healthy. You balance the tires on your car to prevent accidents. You balance your checkbook so you know exactly where you are financially. You know how important it is to keep a balance between work and leisure time to maintain a healthy relationship with those you love. If you lose your balance, you will fall. As important as all these things are, to keep a healthy balance in the rest of your life, you must first be mentally balanced.

I know this because I nearly destroyed my body, had many wrecks, lived in a financial panic, lost those I loved, and fell. I fell into fear, loneliness, despair, and desperation. I fell into addictions and institutions. As long as I remained mentally unbalanced, it was like falling down a deep, black, bottomless hole.

To balance is to bring things into harmony. When you think of harmony, it's natural to think of music. If one note is out of place, if one voice doesn't complement others, if one instrument is out of tune, something that otherwise would have been beautiful becomes a disaster. The same is true for our thought process. When we take our thoughts to inappropriate places, it causes an imbalance. The imbalance leads us to make poor choices. Poor choices take us back to the pit.

Somewhere along my life journey, I was introduced to a concept I call "Flower Power." Flower Power is about finding mental balance through the awareness that there are six places from which we may process our thoughts. The flower is made up of six equal parts, the center plus five petals:

1. Critical parent
2. Nurturing parent
3. Free child
4. Adaptive child
5. Adult
6. Little professor

Each part is essential to good mental health, and the goal is to keep them as equal as possible, as in this "Ideal Flower."

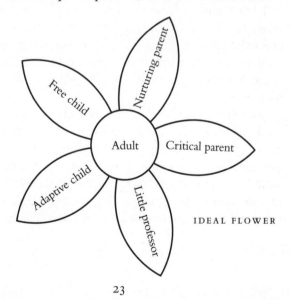

IDEAL FLOWER

The Five Petals of the Flower

CRITICAL PARENT These are the words and teachings of others that live on in your mind. What you were told is right and wrong, how you were punished, and what you were punished for, dwells in this section.

NURTURING PARENT This section is also based on the words and teachings of others. The difference is that it's concerned with kindness, love, and encouragement.

FREE CHILD Imagine climbing a tree without any fear of consequences. Picture yourself jumping in a mud puddle with no worry about your shoes. The free child leaps into life, into situations, without overthinking.

ADAPTIVE CHILD "Okay, if you want me to, I will," is the mantra of the adaptive child. It's that part of you that goes along, hates confrontation, and does whatever is necessary to please others.

ADULT "Let's think this through," says the adult. The adult is analytical. The adult thinks of all the pros and cons of any given situation, and makes a rational decision.

LITTLE PROFESSOR This is the red flag part of the mind. When activated, the little professor shows itself not in what you say or do, but in your true thoughts about whatever is going on.

As I said, each part of the flower is essential for good mental health, but what happens if your wires get crossed and you take your problem, or choice, to the wrong place? Think of a big, red balloon. You blow it up. It's perfect. Squeeze it in the middle and see what happens. When one area gets smaller, other areas get larger. The same thing can happen to your flower.

For instance, let's say that when you were a child, you lived with an extremely critical parent, who punished your free child every time you let it out. One of two things might happen when you are grown. Either the critical parent has squeezed all the life out of your free child, so you are afraid of taking risks, or you will set it free, and jump in where angels fear to tread. Either way is not healthy. There are times and places for you to experience your free child, i.e., when you are playing with your children, on a vacation, relaxing during your leisure time, perhaps when you fall in love. Like the balloon, when one part gets smaller, another must get larger. In this scenario, the critical parent or the free child, grows or diminishes at the expense of the nurturing parent or adaptive child.

Until you become aware of the flower, where the decisions you are making are coming from, you will probably continue to make poor choices. Once you are aware, there is an exercise you can do that will enable you to understand the shape of your flower. The next time you have a decision to make, take six separate sheets of paper and write the name of one of the six parts on each piece. Lay them on the floor in front of you. Ask yourself a question about the choice in front of you. Stand behind each piece of paper and attempt to answer the question from that part of your mind.

After I became aware of the flower, became willing to do the exercise, it helped me understand what happened to change the shape of my flower, my outlook on myself, others, life in general, and the path I chose to travel. At the same time, I realized if I could figure out a way to bring my life, my flower, into balance, there might be hope for me.

For me, harmony is peace, and peace is what I sought. I knew that if I could simply think of my life as a flower and know that the solution lay in the balance of the petals, then

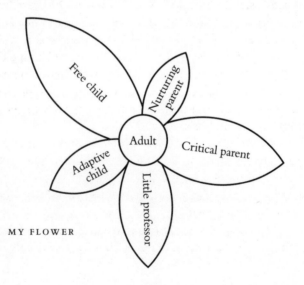

MY FLOWER

26

it was time to take a realistic look at where I was in "My Flower," and how to get where I wanted to be.

Through my life experiences, three of my petals increased, and the center and two petals decreased in size. My balloon got twisted until it looked like a string of link sausages—maybe that's why my thinking was so warped and twisted. I will share with you how I ended up with such an oddly shaped flower.

Nurturing Parent

I don't know if I was an unexpected surprise, simply a disappointment, or my timing was off, but I don't think my arrival was cause for celebration. If it was, it was short-lived. As far back as I can recall, I can't picture anyone in my family holding me, hugging me, or telling me there was anything special about me. My earliest memories are of being either a nuisance or a source of anger. I was in direct competition with a brother that everyone seemed to like. It didn't take me long to figure out the lay of the land. If I were to get any attention, I would have to work for it.

I tried to be good, to do things well, but no matter how hard I tried, it was never good enough. However, I discovered that when I messed up, it got their attention. Any attention, at that time, was better than none. Desperation drove me to extremes.

When I started school and became one of many children fighting for the attention of the teacher, I used the only tool

I had to be special, to get my share of the attention. Each time I behaved badly and got the attention I craved so much that I would do nearly anything for it, my nurturing parent shrunk a little more.

Critical Parent

Remember the balloon. As my nurturing parent got squeezed, twisted, and smaller, my critical parent grew. I surrendered to the only truth I knew. There was something wrong with me. I understood that because so many times those around me would shake their head and say, "There's something wrong with that girl." That's one of the nicer things I heard about myself.

Early on, I learned the touch of a hand was not kind, gentle, or loving, but inappropriate or punishing. Words were used for tearing me down, or trying to control me. I rebelled, but the thoughts and words of those prominent in my life were stuck in my mind. I was bad, and I would never be any better. I became my own critical parent.

Adaptive Child

I was not going to just go along with the rest of the invisible people, do what was expected, blend in with the rest of humanity. If I'd been able to say the truth of the words in my mind, I would have screamed, "Somebody see me.

I'm here. I need you to notice. I need you to care. Please . . . somebody care about me."

I pushed the thoughts way into the back of my brain, and hid the truth of who I believed myself to be behind a mask of arrogance, bluster, and indifference. As much as I would like to say I was not a people pleaser, that I didn't adapt well, I can't because it's not true. I adapted in a different way. I scrutinized every situation and each new person I met, made a decision about what was in it for me, and adapted myself to what I thought they wanted to see and would believe to get whatever it was I desired. I lied, manipulated, conned, and used others.

Justification and rationalization became an art form. I prided myself in fooling others. I told myself if they were that stupid, gullible, emotional, then they deserved whatever they got. I lived by the mantra, "Get them before they get you." As my behavior became more extreme, any part of me that was truly adaptive began to disappear. There was no payoff.

Free Child

The door was open wide for my free child to jump out and run amok, without any consideration for consequences. I could have been the poster child for self-will run riot. I did what I wanted, when I wanted, the way I wanted, and didn't care who I hurt along the way. I went crashing through the world like an angry, hurt child, and if you got in my way, I mowed you down.

If you had something I wanted, I would take it from you, no matter what self-destructive, self-demeaning thing I had to do to get it.

As I look back, I understand that it was the free child part of me that helped me survive, but oh my God, it took me to some bad places, with some really unhealthy people. Once, I ended up in a motel room in Las Vegas, married to a man I barely knew. I didn't even know his last name, and I had it. We were driving his live-in girlfriend's car, who reported it stolen to the police. That's just one example of the way I lived life on a daily basis.

I had the attention span of a gnat. I said whatever I needed to say at the moment to get by. Then, I'd run off on my next great adventure and never give a thought to the wreckage I'd left behind. If you looked at me from the outside, you would think I was having a lot of fun, laughing, joking, being the belle of the ball, but that was not what lived inside. The truth was, I feared stopping, getting off the merry-go-round. If I stopped, faced the truth, grew up, it might kill me. Therefore, I allowed my free child to grow, and grow, and grow.

Little Professor

Let me tell you about when I saw the first red flag in my life. You would have thought it would have been when my first husband left me a few hours after the wedding, or when I found myself married to the man I barely knew. Perhaps it should have been when I buried one child after another, followed closely by my mother's suicide. Maybe it should have been when I was getting beaten regularly. There were so many times, and reasons, but the red flags eluded me.

As long as I stayed drunk, high, or both, I could keep reality at bay. One day, when I was 19 years old, living at a country club on the outskirts of Laramie, Wyoming, where my husband was the golf pro and I ran the pro shop, I was slapped in the face by a red flag. Martin Luther King, Jr. had been killed, and I didn't know it. I awakened, or came to, and had nothing to take the edge off. Appalled that the clubhouse was closed, flag flying at half mast, I drove into town, only to encounter the same thing everywhere. Panic set it. My mind worked furiously. What was I to do?

I located a doctor at a clinic in the closest town, told him I was having an anxiety attack, and got a shot and some pills. I sat thinking in my car outside the clinic. What was wrong with me that I couldn't go one day, one morning, without alcohol or drugs to make the day seem tolerable? Was I addicted? The next thought was, "So what if I am. Given my set of circumstances, anyone would be," as if as long as I had a reason, it was acceptable.

Eventually, the laughter stopped, the fun was no more, and the party was over. If you listened closely, you could hear the sounds of my little professor. My comments became snide and hateful, I criticized others at every given opportunity, thrived on gossip, and enjoyed the misfortune of others. If I could think I was better than one other human being, I could continue down the path I'd chosen. My little professor grew, and showed itself in mean-spirited, ugly ways.

Adult

My critical parent told me I was bad to the bone, and I always would be. My free child took over to enable me to blame others so I could excuse my behavior. My little professor allowed me to strike back at a world I thought had been unfair, with unbridled rage. The only thing I knew about adult thinking was that I had to feed, house, and clothe my son and myself. I fulfilled those duties, although not very well at times. I didn't worry about things like insurance or bills. I figured I could con someone else into taking care of those things, or run away from them. One year, a particularly rough year, I moved thirteen times, just ahead of the law and the landlord. I became adept at middle-of-the-night escapes.

After my oldest son was killed, what few adult thoughts I had left diminished. I figure that, mentally, I hit puberty about the same time I reached menopause. To say I was a late bloomer is an understatement.

I could say I became a strange, exotic flower, but I was mentally unbalanced. I hated myself. I hated others. I blamed everyone and everything, including myself, but I couldn't find a way to change. Flower Power helped me to understand. It gave me power over my mind.

If you find yourself plagued by questions like, "Why am I like this?", "What was I thinking?", "Why did I do that?", "What's wrong with me?", or "How can I figure this out?", you might consider your flower. Draw it out. What does it look like? Why does it look the way it does? What do you need to do to bring it into balance? It's a starting point.

The power of the flower is awareness. You can't change what you don't acknowledge as a problem. You can change the disaster that is your thought process into the beautiful thing it was meant to be. I did.

Changing Words

When does memory begin? Years ago, after I was released from the mental hospital and went to college to study psychology, I was taught that memory begins with the acquisition of verbal skills. I didn't believe that. I believe that even before we are able to express ourselves verbally, the words of others have great impact on us. We don't have to understand the words to comprehend meanings of words through the sound of a voice.

Consider how you train an animal. They have no comprehension of words, no verbal skills, but learn through inflections in your tone of voice what you're trying to get across to them. Can you teach an old dog new tricks? Having worked with many abused animals, some pretty severe, I would, without reservation, say yes.

The difference between humans and the rest of the animal family is that other animals live in the moment, and adjust more easily to change. I had a little terrier, Georgie, who had been starved, beaten, left out in the elements, and thrown out of a car before she came to me. Within a few months, a relatively short period of time considering what she'd endured, I watched her transform into a trusting, sweet, loving dog, content with life. I wondered if, had it been a human that lived through all that she had, how long, if ever, it would have taken that person to heal, to be happy.

For people, it's about memory, and memory is about words and actions that get stuck and clutter up the brain, and the ability to think in a healthy manner. I remember my mom saying, "You never listen. It goes in one ear, and out the other." Ah, if that had only been true. But it wasn't, and it didn't matter if the words I heard were true, but that I accepted them as the truth.

Throughout your life there will be an enormous amount of informational input. All that input from relatives, teachers, friends, enemies, ministers, therapists, etc., will be housed in the brain. How do you sort it all out, get rid of those negatives from the past that are affecting your life today? How do you discern what's true and what's not true? Is it possible to release those old, useless words that have been stuck in your brain for so long? Can you teach mind-cluttered people new tricks?

Let me share with you an exercise I discovered one day while watching television. Because my early life was spent in need and poverty, I've always been fascinated with books and shows that teach people how to do things on their own. I lived in some pretty nasty places, but refused to live badly. I learned the cheapest, most effective ways to kill bugs, clean, decorate, and fix things myself. My limited space forced me to learn organizational skills.

I no longer live in poverty, but I still love to watch home improvement shows. Recently, while considering writing this chapter, I was watching one of my favorite home improvement shows. The host laid three tarps on the lawn in front of a cluttered house, and labeled them, "Keep," "Toss," and "Sell." The occupants of the house, with the help of a team of people, hauled all the clutter out into the light of day, and sorted the items accordingly. Next, the host questioned the owners about each item on the "Keep" tarp to determine why they wished to hang on to it.

My mind wandered to my writing. Since this chapter is concerned with thoughts and words, wouldn't it be great if we could do to the cluttered mind what the TV host was doing to that house? Why not? We could develop our own show, and call it "Changing Words." The set would be a brain enlarged to the size of a house, cluttered with words— stacks of words that define who you believe yourself to be, words bequeathed to you from others, antique words that hold memories of the past, and old discarded words that haven't been used in some time because you could no longer live up to them.

I am a visual person, so I drew a picture of my brain house before I cleared away the clutter, and opened the door to a new way of thinking.

In my illustration, the door to my brain house is closed because I had a closed mind. There is a pile of words directly in front of the door. They are the words that defined me. Some were bequeathed to me, others I picked up along the way. Any new thought I had that tried to squeeze through a crack in the door, every decision I made, had to be filtered through this stack of words.

Beyond the stack by the door is my overflowing trash can filled with words I'd thrown away. They were words I couldn't live up to, so I trashed them. Floating above are the words I used to excuse the way I thought and acted.

In the back of my brain house are the words that constantly haunted me. No matter where I went, what I did, who I was with, they were there. They were there to ruin every relationship in my life, to throw me into night terrors, to catapult me into one addiction after another.

The words at the bottom are the ones I figured I would take to my grave. Anyone who knew me back when I was addicted would have told you I would probably be dead before I reached the age of 30. Considering the words that cluttered my brain, it was not that far-fetched. But, live I did, and at 35 decided it was time to clean house, starting with my brain.

When I became willing to open the door and allowed others to help me clear out the mess and lay it out on three tarps, we came up with the following.

KEEP	EXCHANGE	TRASH
Stupid	Ugly	Integrity
Failure	Crazy	Self-esteem
Worthless	Alone	Self-respect
Angry	Misfit	Peace
Selfish		Hope
Addict		Power
Victim		Spiritual
Afraid		Daughter
Enraged		Wife
Confused		Mother
Loser		
Idiot		

Can you believe my "Keep" tarp? You're probably wondering why anyone would hold on so tightly to those words. They kept me from taking responsibility for my actions, allowed me to remain a child, and kept the expectations of others away. Like the wall of addictions I put up between myself and the world, these words were for protection.

Because I chose to keep certain words in my life, other words were sacrificed. That would be my "Trash" pile. There is no way to hang on to both. Have you ever known a failure with self-esteem, a selfish person with integrity, or an angry person with peace?

There were a few words on my "Exchange" tarp. I thought if I could appear better, I would be better; if I stayed with others, I wouldn't be lonely; if I could act sane, others wouldn't realize there was something mentally wrong with me; and, someday, some way, I would find a way to push myself into a world where I'd always been a square peg in a round hole. The words laid out, in the light of day for everyone to see, helped me understand I couldn't change what I couldn't see. It was time to play "Changing Words."

To play the game, you must be willing to pick up each word on the "Keep" tarp, and answer those all-important questions.

- Where did you get it?
- What does it mean to you?
- Do you use it?
- How do you use it?
- When was the last time you used it?
- Why do you think you need it?
- What would your life be like without it?

Let's take the first word on my "Keep" tarp, "Stupid," and apply these questions to it.

- Where did I get it?
  From my parents, other relatives, and teachers, who compared me to my highly intelligent older brother; I never measured up.

- What does it mean to me?
  It means, why bother, why try?

- Do I use it?
  You bet. I use it regularly.

- How do I use it?
  To avoid making efforts that will only end in failure?

- When was the last time I used it?
  When I had an opportunity for a better job that could have changed my life, but would have required me to meet certain expectations . . . like being sober.

- Why do I think I need it?
  To avoid expectations and disappointments.

- What would my life be like without it?
  This was the question to ponder. What "would" my life be like if I didn't believe I was stupid? I might actually be willing to try to succeed, to risk failure, and know that failure is not in the trying without success, but in the not trying.

In "Changing Words," each word, on each tarp, taken out, questioned, and explored, can be moved to another, more appropriate tarp. As I played "Changing Words," I came to understand what it meant to clear the clutter of the mind.

Now it's your turn to be the contestant. Draw a picture of your brain house and show all the clutter that lives there.

Consider each word carefully as you place it.

Imagine I am the host of the show. We are standing together on the "Keep" tarp, and I'm asking you the previ-

KEEP	EXCHANGE	TRASH

ously listed questions about the clutter that you insist on keeping. How would you explain it to me? Move on to the next two tarps, and repeat the process.

There's a drum roll. It's time for you to play "Changing Words." If you've answered the questions honestly, you'll know exactly where each word belongs. Where will you put them?

KEEP	EXCHANGE	TRASH

You might think it's silly to write the words in a big brain house and on tarps, and to answer the questions out loud as if you are explaining your answers to me, but there is something about seeing things in black and white and hearing the words verbalized that makes them seem more real. The point of the imaginary show is to face reality head on, to become aware of the clutter that holds you back, and to understand the choice to change the words is within your power.

Does it work? It worked for me. By being brutally honest, willing to answer the hard questions, and willing to expose the truth to the light of day, I changed the words that changed my life.

Don't Miss Your Ride

Travel broadens the mind and horizons. Each new place, person, food, language, or experience stimulates the mind to let it know there is more out there. Knowing there is more out there allows you to open the gates to the boundaries that keep you from expanding your horizons. To expand your horizon means to enlarge your range of perception about the world, others, and yourself.

There are travelers, pedestrians, and runners. I was a runner. I moved fast, lived many places, encountered people from all walks of life, tasted foods and drinks, and lived through one experience after another. However, for all I learned, I might as well have been sitting in a darkened bar, in Nowhere, USA, with blinders, earmuffs, and tape over my mouth. My horizon stretched as far as the back bar, and the amber liquid that was one of the boundaries that wouldn't allow me any forward progression.

Like the snail pulls into its shell when it perceives danger, real or imagined, I pulled into my mind. It was a dark place, filled with fear-based thoughts and nasty words, where I could use self-pity to justify and rationalize the way I lived.

Running doesn't always involve the feet. One thing about the brain is that it was always with me, on site, for a fast escape.

Inside my alcohol-soaked, drugged brain, my mind convinced me that I didn't want to be a pedestrian, simply standing by the side of the road, watching the world go by. It lied, and told me what I was doing was better. I remember thinking that I didn't want to die in bed, but wanted to go out with a flash, in some exciting way—a way that others would talk about and remember. Then I'd have another drink and float away into some delusional world where I had quickly become a legend in my own mind.

I convinced myself I was a traveler rather than a runner. God knows I'd moved all over the place, most times in a hurry. I'd experienced giving birth, surviving deaths, marriages, divorces, numerous jobs, every mode of transportation, from hitchhiking to airplanes, and was in reality nothing more than a fast-moving pedestrian. It's like I was standing on the side of the road, running in place as fast as I could, as the world passed me by.

Occasionally, a new word or idea would slip into my closed, cluttered mind, and fly around like a gnat, agitating, aggravating, forcing me to pay attention. It usually happened when I reached moments of desperation, and a crack appeared in my guarded mind. Some of the words that sneaked in were "change," "solutions," and most of all, "help!" I couldn't do it on my own. I needed help.

The choice was mine. I could either go down in flames, or ask for help. As much as I told myself I didn't care if I died, when the moment came, I made a phone call. Little did I know that one call to a 12-step program would change my life forever. In the meetings, I encountered real travelers; people who were on a journey I had yet to experience. I wanted to go, but wasn't sure if I had the willingness to get prepared or the courage to step off the curb and take the ride.

At first, it was a rough ride, but I soon discovered I was not alone. There was always a hand there to steady me when I would have fallen. With each step I took, the door to my mind opened a little wider, not only to let new thoughts in, but also to release those thoughts that were holding me back. After a time, my horizon was like looking at the vastness of the ocean. My life was enormous, with no limitations, no boundaries, except the ones that were self-imposed. It was time to become a traveler, to challenge myself every day, to see, hear, taste, and experience all that life had to offer, and savor each moment.

It's important to ask yourself if you are running in place, telling yourself you are a traveler, and getting nowhere, standing by the side of the road watching the world go by, or if you are a traveler, progressing forward. If you're a runner, racing through a maze like a lab rat, bumping into one dead end after another, wouldn't it simply be smart to take the hand of another, who knows the way out, and let that person lead you? It doesn't matter if it's a 12-step program, a religious setting, therapy, or counseling. Do yourself a favor; stop and ask for help.

If you are standing by the side of the road, watching life pass you by, don't kid yourself—it is a choice. I have known people confined to wheelchairs, with limited mobility, who are great travelers, and others with total mobility who might as well have been paralyzed. Traveling is about engaging in life—every aspect of it. Your body doesn't have to move for your mind to progress forward.

If you want to be a traveler, you have that choice. With willingness and courage, there will be no limits on your horizon. If I could tell you one thing, give you one gift, it would be, "Don't miss your ride." It will be the ride of your life, worth every effort you are willing to make. Stop hiding in your head, wading through cluttered words from the past that have nothing to do with you today. Take hold of an offered hand of an experienced traveler, and ride with that person until you can ride on your own. Someday you will be the training wheels that will steady another until he or she is ready to become a traveler.

TIPS FOR KEEPING IT SIMPLE AND SANE

- Thoughts can accumulate like old, dusty house clutter, and provide you with an excuse not to move forward with your life, but to dwell in the familiar.

- Quit thinking about what you "should" have done. If you could have done it differently, you would have.

- You must first be mentally balanced to achieve a total healthy balance in your life. You can use the Flower Power concept to measure how mentally balanced you are and to make healthier choices.

- Consider words that you believe define you, words you have heard others use to describe you, words that come from past memories, and old words that might once have been used to describe you. Are there words you are holding on to that caused you to sacrifice other, more positive words? You have the power to change those words, but it's a choice you have to make for yourself.

- Engage in every aspect of life that you can, and enjoy the ride. Accept the helping hands of travelers who have gone before you, and when you become a traveler, be ready to offer your own hand to those that need guidance in their own rides.

Keep
It
Emotionally
Simple

The deeper that sorrow
Carved into your being
The more joy you can contain.

—Kahlil Gibran

Fight or Flee

When faced with a dangerous situation, all animals are endowed with the instinct to fight or flee. No matter how evolved humans have become, we are, after all, still a part of the animal family, and we share that same basic instinct. This not only applies to the fear of physical danger, but also to anything that could be hazardous to our health, even our emotional well-being.

Cave dwellers used this instinct to escape predatory animals that were going to devour them until, being the problem solvers of the animal kingdom, they figured out a way to fight back.

It's not that far-fetched to imagine being engulfed, or devoured, by emotions that trigger fear. Using common items, our forerunners built weapons to fight and tools to survive. The key was to understand who they were, what they were capable of, who or what the enemy was, and how to fight back. I wonder if they thought, "I'm walking upright, I'm smarter, and I don't want to run away and hide anymore."

We may not be running into caves to avoid perceived dangers, but we do know what it is to flee. The great escape from life's problems can be seen through avoidance, distraction, and addictions. The more evolved we've become, the more inventive we've become in the ways of escape. It's much easier than fighting back, but allows our fears to live on; to devour us.

As far back as I can remember, I was baffled by everything. It seemed like everyone else knew the big secret to life, and no one was telling me. I had all these feelings with no clue what to do with them. I watched. I listened. I thought that if I emulated those around me, maybe I'd discover their secret.

My brother, a year older than I was, always had his nose stuck in a book or was working on homework. That wouldn't work for me. I was stupid. I knew I was because I was told so often. I hated school. Dad worked on the railroad, and when he wasn't gone, he drank whiskey and slept. Since he needed absolute quiet, or else the leather strap would come out, my mother would take us on outings. Sometimes we would go to a farm where mom's friend lived. We were shuffled outside so she could visit with her friend. I didn't like him. I didn't like it there. I didn't understand why we couldn't go in the house.

Other times, she met her friend at her brother's apartment. There was an old record player for us to listen to while they were in the bedroom "visiting." Again, we were not allowed inside. When she emerged from the inner sanctum, disheveled, smelling funny, she would remind us that we must never tell our father where we'd been, or about her secret friend.

Dad must have figured something out, because through the thin walls of the small, clapboard house, I heard them fighting. I was scared all the time. However, I knew the punishment for crying was a whipping. I never quite figured that out. When I got a whipping with the belt, if I cried, they said they would give me something to cry about if I didn't shut up. I thought they already had.

I definitely had the instinct to fight my situation, but when I did, I got knocked down one way or another. Everything I did seemed to be wrong. Unable to express what I felt, I learned to harbor my hate, my anger, my rage, my resentments, and told myself that someday, some way, I would escape and never come back. Where was a cave when I needed one?

Things changed, but not for the better. We moved to a nicer house, and dad's brother moved in with us. There were always people at the new house, relatives from both sides, and friends, but not mom's secret friend. Cigarette smoke wafted through the house, beer bottles lay on the floor like dead soldiers, there was a lot of laughter, and they all seemed to like each other . . . really like each other. Sometimes I peeked through the bedroom door, and watched the grown-ups doing the strangest things. I was confused. I was frightened. What if one of them came in my bedroom? What if they did things to me? My fear was realized before

I started the third grade. After that, when there were people over, I huddled under my bed, afraid to go to sleep.

Suddenly, my dad was gone, and had been replaced by his brother; a formidable man with cold eyes, and the rigidity he'd learned in the army. I'd gone from being ignored or punished, depending on what I was up to, to being expected to be a little soldier. There were rules—lots of rules, and I broke them all. I just couldn't seem to get the hang of it. I was angry, and I did everything I could to make my mother and her new husband miserable. I fought back, but I never really won. I ran away to escape, but they always found me. Every day, every thought revolved around escape. I pictured my dad sitting all alone, drunk and sad.

He wasn't alone. In no time he'd remarried, and had a stepdaughter that was everything I wasn't. I hated all of them.

When my mother's friend reappeared, and the fighting began again, mom found a solution to her problems. If she mixed these little green and white pills with her booze, all the fear and pain disappeared, at least for a while. I will never forget the feeling I got the first time I sneaked into her medicine cabinet and took one of the pills. It was the escape I'd been searching for all along. I drifted into the land of oblivion. I was tired of fighting, of struggling with feelings that had no answers. If it was fight or flee, I chose to flee.

I ran away from everything, because everything, every-one, and my feelings filled me with fear. I told myself it was about survival. I survived, but I paid the price. I was afraid to love because I might get hurt, so I cheated myself out of every relationship in my life, even with my children. I was afraid to mourn because it might overwhelm me, so I carried my pain like a yoke around my neck until it drove me to addictions and finally a mental hospital. I was afraid of anything good happening in my life because when it ended, the pain and anger would be triggered again. I even became afraid to go to sleep at night because that was the one time I had no control, and no way to run away. It all began when I surrendered to fear as a child.

Think back over your own life, and figure out when you made the decision to fight or flee, and the ramifications that may still be with you today. It probably wasn't a red-letter day, and there was no burning bush, but you either quietly surrendered or you powered yourself up for the fight. If, like me, you gave in to the fear, what forms of escape did you use? Did you throw yourself into a career at the exclusion of all else because it was safer? What did you give up? Have you failed at one relationship after another, all the time telling yourself it was about the others involved, that nobody "gets" you? Did you realize you were the one common denominator in the equation? Have you fallen into addictions and reassured yourself that you can handle it . . . that it's not really a problem? What is it you give up every day to feed that addiction? Do you isolate, hold yourself away from the world and other people, and wonder why you are lonely and uninvolved? Do you stay busy, busy, busy, run here and there, doing this and that, with the belief that as long as you don't stop, you don't have to see the truth of who you are and how you feel, and wonder why you suffer from exhaustion?

On the other hand, did you decide to fight? There are both healthy and unhealthy ways to fight. What did you choose? To fight in an unhealthy manner, you must adapt the "killer" instinct. You will believe that life is unfair, people are out to get you, and therefore whatever you do, in whatever way, is justified. Phrases such as "The end justifies the means," "Get them before they get you," "They deserve whatever they get," "I'm just doing what I have to do," will be your mantras. What is the price of fighting dirty? Someday, as you travel along the path that is your life, you will run into a mirror. The mirror could be held up by your children, a tragic event, or simply unhappiness, but it will be in a place where you can't go around it. It is the mirror of truth. What will you see?

The healthier way to fight back is through an internal struggle. What, or who, is the enemy, the problem? How do you feel about it, them? Why? What is it about the person or situation that affects you? Does it have anything to do with past experiences? Do you have all the facts? Can you change the person or situation, or must you change your perception? How much of your time, effort, and peace are you willing to give up for the situation? The healthy fighter will see the situation from all angles, look inward for their part in the problem, get in touch with their feelings, figure out why they feel that way, and then act accordingly. They have discovered that not reacting is more important than any action they can take.

What is the key to keeping it emotionally simple? You are responsible, not only for your thoughts and actions, but your feelings as well. It is your responsibility to figure out what is holding you back in life, and to do whatever it takes to fix it.

When you are emotionally cluttered by feelings from the past that you have held on to for years, there is no room for the new. All situations and people are unique. When you judge either by your past experience, who pays the price? You are the one who has cheated yourself out of a new experience because of fear. You may feel safe, but your journey is like standing in a minefield. As long as you stand still, you won't get hurt. At the same time, you will never know the freedom and lightness of being able to walk through the world unfettered and unafraid. You can exist in the minefield, or you can find a blueprint and risk walking through it. It's entirely up to you.

Unintended Consequences

There is a cliché about the ripple effect. You throw a pebble into calm water and watch the ripples until they reach shore. In other words, for every action, there is a reaction. Let's take that a bit further. Imagine throwing a rock into the surging waves of the ocean. You may not see the ripple or understand the effect, but that doesn't mean it doesn't exist.

The rock displaced a certain amount of water; it could become home to tiny sea creatures, may have landed on something and killed it, or hit a fish on the way down, causing it damage. You didn't mean for any of those things to happen. They are unintended consequences.

Life is a series of interesting events; pebbles thrown into the pond. Each event will elicit not only thought, but also emotion. They may come from the same place, but are very far apart. Logically, you understand that for every decision you make, there will be consequences. What of the emotional choices you make?

Do you think there won't be consequences, even unintended consequences? I'm reasonably certain I was an unintended consequence of young, raging hormones, masked as love. Ah, love—it's considered the strongest emotion humans possess. It's also the scapegoat emotion, used as an excuse to justify all forms of strange behavior, from indiscriminate, unsafe sex to murder. Talk about unintended consequences. You can't imagine that all babies are planned, that people end up with diseases, get divorced, commit crimes of passion, or live in misery as part of their plan for life. It wasn't what I expected, nor do I think it was what my parents expected.

However, because of my parents' unintended consequences, I became a victim. As an unwanted, unloved child, I believed there was something wrong with me. If my own parents couldn't love me, who could? I yearned for physical contact, for someone to tell me I was worthy. It didn't take me long to locate men who would help me out with that. I prefaced each encounter by convincing myself I was in love, and that they loved me. I didn't have the vaguest idea what it meant to love or be loved, but it seemed like the answer to my needs.

And, the ripples continued when my unintended consequence was born. I was an emotionally stunted child with a baby, which did not bode well for the baby. I finally knew what it was to be loved, but the ability to understand loving another, putting that person's needs above my own, eluded me.

I grabbed hold of this loving little boy, and dragged him through the gutter that was my life. When my other children died, when I fell into addictions, had brief encounters with men, some of whom I married and divorced, I was emotionally unavailable to him. Hell, I was emotionally unavailable to myself. I could not see past my own nose; feel past my own pain. I gave no thought to where the ripples were headed and how they affected others.

I didn't care that some married man, whom I told myself I was in love with, had a wife and family. If I didn't have to see it, it wasn't real in my life. Today, I understand that just because I didn't see it, didn't mean it didn't exist. What I did had ramifications, not only for my child and me, but for others as well.

As ripples have a way of doing, mine hit the shore, and returned to the point of origin. That would be me. I remember my grandmother saying, "What goes around, comes around." I didn't know what that meant until much later in life. For a period of time, I tried to get my life together, but by then, the "what comes around" showed itself in my son. Helplessly, I watched him becoming me. I tried to help, to change things, but I had left it too late. He was killed before that happened.

I am not trying to justify or excuse anything I've done. I simply want you to understand that even though you may have the best of intentions, sometimes there are unintended consequences. I recall thinking before I got into my self-destructive lifestyle that I would never be like my parents, that if I ever had children, it would be different. I hated what alcohol and pills did to them. I would never drink or take drugs. When I met Mr. Right, it would be forever. There would be no fighting, no abuse, no messing around with others. I did every one of those things, and more, and all in the name of love, or lack of love.

There will be a point in every person's life when he or she will be faced with the decisions made, the consequences, and the unintended consequences. For some, it may not come until the point of death. For others, like me, the truth will come home to visit before it's too late. I know I am one of the lucky ones, although it didn't feel like it at the time. The person staring back at me in my life mirror was not pretty. It would take years, and a lot of help, to change.

You may be wondering how one changes unintended consequences. It begins by paying attention to the ripples, by getting out of yourself enough to understand the choices you make today could affect not only you, but also others, for years, even decades. How many times have you seen it in other families, possibly your own? One generation after another of emotionally unstable people, who keep passing the trait on.

It's difficult to be the person who breaks the cycle. It will not be appreciated by many family members and friends. That's because you become the mirror. When you try to get your life together, to do better, every time they see you, it forces them to see a little more of the truth.

Recently, I saw a television commercial that hit home. It showed one person helping another, then, when that person had the opportunity to help someone else, he did it, and that person helped another person, and so on. The first person who helped would never see where the ripple ended up, but it was her pebble in the pond that began the cycle of events that followed. That's how you change unintended consequences.

When you simply do the next right thing, you will stop worrying about the consequences, and when you no longer have to worry about consequences, there is no need to worry about unintended consequences. There may be times when you will have to put your feelings aside, or examine your emotions, to help another. It means taking a risk. The risk is about getting involved in life—the lives of others, and your own.

If, like me, you have the need to feel loved, it's important to understand that you will never feel loved until you believe you are lovable. As long as you keep throwing negative pebbles into the pond, you will not attract the true affection you desire. Even if you do, you will not be able to accept it, which will again lead to unintended consequences.

I started out as a product of negative unintended consequences, and ended up the person I am today through the unintended consequences of a ripple that began over seventy years ago. When two men, with the same problem, came together to support each other, and that idea grew into a 12-step program, they had no idea their concept would one day save the lives of millions, including me.

If you are emotionally disabled because you've stuffed your true emotions away until they've crippled you, it's time to become an investigator. Take a realistic look backward. What ripples were set in motion, perhaps before you were born, that swept you along? How has that affected the person you are, the choices you've made?

You may think you know the predominant people in your life, but I'll bet there is a lot you don't know about them. Sometimes when I'm working with young women, I know they can't imagine I was ever young, thin, and struggling through the same problems. It takes sharing my story, being open and honest in answering any questions they have, to help them understand we are not that different. The best way to find out the truth is to ask questions, and listen ... really listen. Listen not only with your ears, but with your heart.

When I finally stopped constantly thinking about myself, I began to hear. I always wondered why my father hadn't been there for me, at least emotionally. I knew the story of his mother's death; it had come up over the years. However, I didn't really hear it until I became willing to listen. One day, I decided to ask him what happened. Although I hadn't had a strong bond with him as a father, that day, I bonded with the unsure, frightened, hurt, angry little boy that had lived through so much.

My heart pictured him, the youngest of five children, in the midst of the Depression, scrambling for enough food to eat. As if his life wasn't hard enough, there was a house fire. His mother was burned, but didn't die immediately. The children were taken to the hospital to see her one last time before she finally succumbed.

I will never forget what he said to me. He said, "It was like she'd melted. I still have nightmares about her." His father nearly lost his mind, began to drink heavily, and took his anger out on the children. By the time I came along, my grandfather was already up in years, and had another wife. I couldn't imagine the man I knew could ever hurt a child, but I don't doubt that it was the truth. Little by little, as my father's story unfolded, I began to understand the ripple effect that changed the path of his life, the person he might have been.

What I understand now is that we all begin life with generations of ripples, choices made before we were even born, that can affect our lives. What can we do about it? I said, "It stops here. It ends with me. The time to take a stand is now." I stepped back from myself, asked questions, listened, and found some compassion for others, and finally for myself.

Before you toss that pebble into the pond, or rock into the ocean, stop and think about the consequences, the possible unintended consequences. The ripples you cause today could last for generations. Whether you see the results or not, you are responsible. Once aware, there is no excuse left to continue along the same path. From this day forward, you have a choice. You can change things, one pebble at a time.

Time: The Great Healer?

When tragedies took my breath away, trauma brought me low, and even when I got into recovery from addiction, there was one phrase repeated frequently by well-meaning individuals: "Time is the great healer."

Years passed and time did not heal my emotional wounds. If anything, they grew and festered. Outwardly, I seemed to be tough, indifferent, able to survive anything life threw at me, but inside, I was like one huge exposed nerve waiting to be touched by someone. Then, I could lash out and justify my behavior.

I thrived on the three "Rs," and I'm not talking about reading, writing, and arithmetic. My three "Rs" were resentment, rage, and revenge. I resented everyone who caused me pain, who didn't understand my pain, who had anything I didn't, and who I couldn't bring down to my level. I swallowed my feelings, pushed them down, until they became a big ball of rage that lived within. There was ample opportunity, real or imagined, every day, to add to the rage. I could take the most innocent comment and turn it into something awful. When anyone did or said something that triggered my emotions, I took it as a personal insult. My obsession with revenge kept the feelings away and gave me a sense of meaning in my otherwise pathetic life. If I could cause you pain, I felt powerful. As powerless as I'd felt my entire life, I grabbed any power I could, any way I could.

No, time had not healed my wounds. No matter how many years passed or how old I was, inside lived a hurt little girl filled with fear of rejection, of abandonment, and of never knowing what it meant to love or be loved.

At age 35, I hit rock bottom with my addictions. It was do or die time. My choices were either a dead end or the long road to recovery. I wish I could tell you why or how I chose the road to recovery, but I really don't know. The only thing I can come up with is that, for some unknown reason, I didn't want to die. I don't know why. I'd lost everyone important in my life either to death or disgust, most of my possessions, and it certainly wasn't about religious beliefs. If there was a God in my life, I was unaware.

I convinced myself I simply needed to rest, to sit among others like me who had suffered greatly and turned to the numbing substances that made life tolerable. I had no idea what recovery entailed. I soon learned that just putting in my time would not fix me. A lovely older woman, who looked like she would never put anything nasty in her mouth, informed me the day would come in recovery when I would hit my emotional bottom. I was skeptical. What did this woman, who looked like someone's granny, know about it? When she spoke during the meeting, however, I sat in my chair absolutely stunned. She'd lived a life that rivaled my own and exceeded it in some ways. I panicked!

For nearly a year, I attended meetings, spent time with others in recovery, listened to their stories, and became physically stronger, but continued to keep a tight rein on my emotions. One day, that changed. A young man shared his name and addiction. My head jerked around. My heart stopped momentarily as I looked into familiar hazel eyes and saw that crooked smile I remembered so well. He was the best friend of my son, who had passed away nearly six years earlier. A hand touched my back, and the person across the table pushed a box of tissues toward me. I didn't even realize tears were pouring down my face.

My mind drifted to the past, to a time when the boys were little and played in my backyard. I could watch them out the kitchen window as they romped, played cowboys and army men, and pushed dump trucks through the dirt. There was an old root cellar with a grape arbor that they used for their fort, boys club, and hideout.

One day, it seemed as if they'd been in the root cellar all afternoon. I decided to check on them. The two boys were in the cellar with soda bottles, bunches of green grapes, and sheepish grins. I asked what they were doing. Between mumbling and the shuffling of feet, I discerned that they were squeezing the juice out of the green grapes into the empty bottles, and making wine. It took me a moment to realize there was no way they'd gotten that much juice out of the amount of grapes they'd picked. Their "wine" was a mixture of grapes and urine, and they were planning to sell it to the neighborhood kids.

And, there was my son's friend, sitting in a meeting with me because he suffered from addiction; I couldn't help but feel somewhat responsible. Flooded with memories and feelings, I wept. Back then I didn't cry, at least not in front of others. I considered crying a weakness, and I knew what happened to weak people. They got chewed up and spit out, like my mother, who killed herself at the age of 39. But when I saw my son's best friend and heard him speak about his addictions, I wept from the deepest part of my soul, from a place where shame, guilt, despair, great sorrow, and loss lived.

Have you ever had a moment in your life when the tears came suddenly, with a force over which you had no control? I think it's like filling a glass of water one drip at a time. Slowly, the emotions drip into your body, stay there as long as they remain unexpressed, and one day, you are full to overflowing. The problem is that there are not enough tears to wash away the clutter of emotions that have accumulated. It will take decisive action.

If you are saying to yourself that you are fine, that you just won't think about those things that hurt you, you need to understand that those painful feelings continue to live in that secret, dark place where you don't allow anyone to go, and rarely visit yourself. It's like having a room in your house that's dim, dirty, trashed, and cluttered. You may not go into the room, but you know it's there. You know there is a mess hiding just beyond the closed door. When someone comes to visit, you keep the door closed as protection from their judgment.

The same thing occurs when a new person enters your life. You may want a relationship, friendship, or to love and be loved, but you feel that you must keep them out at all costs, even if it means losing a person you desire in your life. You must keep the door closed for fear they will see who you really are. It's difficult to have healthy, long-lasting relationships when you are constantly on guard.

With that in mind, and if you are willing to open the door to your cluttered emotions, the first thing to determine is the difference between your secret emotional identity and whom you pretend to be publicly. I discovered a simple exercise that can help you make that distinction.

I call this exercise the "T-Shirt Experiment." I'm fascinated by T-shirts embellished with words and pictures; what they say about the wearer. Think of the T-shirts you've worn over the years. As you've changed, they've changed. This exercise can show you exactly where you are at this moment. You will be the designer. On the front of your T-shirt, in pictures, words, or both, you will depict what you wish others to see, and on the back, the truth of who you are. As an example, the design I did before I got into recovery from my emotional clutter had the words "Beware! Alligator Mouth" on the front and "Caution! Hummingbird Heart" on the back, with corresponding animal drawings.

I chose an alligator for the front of my T-shirt because I wanted you to believe I was tough, that nothing could penetrate my alligator hide and get to my soft underbelly. The words tell you to step back, and not to get too close, or you'll pay. Like the gator, you never know when I will snap and bite your head off. Of course, it was all smoke and mirrors to protect the truth as shown on the back of my T-shirt.

The hummingbird on the back tells you about my tiny, fragile heart, which is easily damaged, and that I move quickly, flying here and there, never landing in one place too long for fear of being hurt.

Keeping up the gator pretense for so many years was wearing and hurtful, not only to me, but to others who wanted to be a part of my life as well. I found that the first step to clearing out the emotional clutter that continually kept me in conflict was to open the door, look at my mess, and understand that as long as it was there, it influenced who I was, how I lived, and every relationship in my life.

What will your T-shirt look like? How do you present yourself to the world on the front? What design will you use on the back to tell the truth? Why does it matter? It matters because you matter. It matters because there are others involved, be it family, friends, coworkers, even those you have yet to meet. It matters because whether you believe it or not, whether you want to be or not, we are all in this together and we touch each others' lives.

After you've chosen your designs, consider them. How different are they? What do they tell you about yourself? Are you hiding your feelings under a tough exterior as I did? Are you an emotional clutter junkie? If so, how can you clean up the mess? After you clean it up, how can you keep from repeating the same scenario?

You've made a start when you acknowledge the problem. Say it out loud. That makes it more real. Only when you admit something is real and has a negative effect on you will you begin the healing process. Like any other clutter, it will be a matter of examination and choices. Just as you would pick up an item of clothing from the floor, examine it, and ask yourself why you have it, if you need it, if it will fit, and what its value is to you, so you should do with emotions. If you choose to hold onto a particular feeling, it's filling some need.

Imagine you pick up shame and guilt. Where did you get them? Why are you keeping them? What value do they have? The shame and guilt I had stashed away began to collect into corners when I was a child. Things happened to me. I kept the secrets. I blamed myself. I should have been able to fight back, to take a stand. As unrealistic as it was to imagine I had any control over being victimized by adults, I continued to carry that burden for many years. That became my base excuse for self-destructive behavior and self-imposed limitations. As long as I kept adding to the pile, keeping it behind a closed door, I would never have to strive for a successful, happy life, and risk failure.

Take another look at your T-shirt, front and back. The object of the exercise is to bring the two sides together so you are one person. Drag out those emotions depicted on the front of your shirt, ask the pertinent questions, answer them honestly, and then imagine what life would be without them. If anger is part of your clutter, when did it start? Who or what was the cause? What did you do about it? Did you have any part in the situation?

Do you think your anger has affected another person? How has it affected you? When you dissect the situation, do you discern things you could have done differently? Is there anything you need to do today, i.e., make an apology, a financial restitution, or perhaps leave a door open for amends and forgiveness? My guess is that the situation has passed, and the other person involved has either resolved it or it wasn't that important to them in the first place, so they've forgotten about it. You would be the one causing yourself sleepless nights, headaches, and emotional stress as you wallow in an emotional mud pit until you are stuck fast. The anger owns you, is in control.

The only way to regain control over an emotion is to resolve what triggered it and spring into action, doing whatever it takes to change what you can, accept what you can't change, know you did everything within your power, and then let it go. It no longer serves any useful purpose.

Even after you've cleared away the emotional clutter that is causing limitations in your life, emotional situations will continue to happen. Life is like that. To avoid rebuilding the clutter, you must deal with each situation as it arises and understand that every circumstance is unique. You cannot judge one by another. Allow yourself to feel what you are feeling when you are feeling it. You can cry about it, talk about it, but more importantly, you should realize that it's not forever if you are willing to face it, deal with it, and take action. It's not a bad thing to feel deeply, unless you tuck it in that dark place and allow it to continue having impact on your life.

I told you what my T-shirt looked like before I found a better way. Today, it would look the same on both sides. I would do a picture of a big smile, with the words "Happy, Joyous, and Free" beneath it. I am happy and joyous because I'm free of the emotional clutter that nearly destroyed my life, and because I refuse to let it build up again by taking care of business promptly.

What would you like your T-shirt to say about you? Remember, you are the designer.

You and Your Karma

Karma is normally associated with reincarnation, and the concept that what you've done in former lives and what you do in this life will determine your journey toward your destiny in your life, or lives, to come. What if that were true? What if this is it; your last life . . . your last hurrah?

Karma is about motivation. It's not as important what you do, or how you do it, but why you make a specific choice, and the truth of the feelings behind that choice. If you are wealthy and donate a lot of money to a cause but are doing it for a tax-write-off, does it take anything away from the good the money can do? No. Your motive, however, will say a lot about what is important to you. If you have ten dollars left, and you walk past a homeless person, or you encounter a person in need and can empathize, feel their pain, and give them the last of your money, you have not only enhanced their life, but your own.

You may be thinking that it's much more important for a person to give a million dollars to cancer research than it is to hand a hungry man a sandwich, but to me, as gifts, they are equal. If you have never known hunger, that gnawing feeling deep in your gut, the effort it takes to move, the inability to think of anything but food, then it's difficult to understand the value of a sandwich.

I don't know if there have been other lives, but I know that things that happened in this life have impacted my perception, my choices, and most certainly my motives. There were many years when I could not recognize the gifts I received. These gifts are not what you would think of in the usual sense. What are they?

1. **CHILDREN** Yes, my children died, but even if I'd known ahead of time all the pain of loss I would suffer, I would have had them, would not have given up one moment in time with them. I know others who are not capable of having children who would give anything for the experience. The gifts I received from this are the understanding that life is fragile and not to be wasted, and having experienced the pain of great loss enables me to help others who are suffering. When I say, "I understand," they know it's true.

2. **MY MOTHER** She shot herself and died when I was still in my teens. Her suicide kept me alive for years. I did not want to leave my one living child feeling about me the way I did about her. Watching her suffer in an unhappy marriage but consumed with fear of the unknown that drove her to the grave taught me how not to live. After one experience with marital abuse, I escaped, never to let things get

to that point again. The gift was to hold on to life no matter what, and never give in to abuse. Anything the unknown holds is better than being beaten down mentally, emotionally, or physically.

3. **STRANGERS** I moved frequently. I worked many jobs, sometimes several at a time. Because I had very little bond with family, much of my life was spent with strangers. I call them my earthbound angels. As a single, teenaged mother living hand to mouth, you can only imagine some of the scrapes I got into. Once, when I'd escaped from the abusive husband, I found myself, along with my 4-year-old son, on a bus with no money. I'd packed a bread bag full of bacon sandwiches, and filled a thermos with tea. I have no idea why I thought that would get us through a three-day trip. By the end of the second day there was nothing left. When I'd just about decided I'd either have to beg for money or steal at the next bus stop, three sailors got on the bus, and sat directly in front of us. My son made friends with them. Like me, he'd never met a stranger. The three young men said they would watch him if I wanted to sleep a while. I was so tired, I agreed. He must have told them we were out of food. After that, every time the bus stopped, they took him in and bought him food, and brought me coffee and sandwiches. They got off one stop before ours, and I've never

seen them again. But, for that one day, they were the angels that saved us. Throughout many hard times in my life, strangers have shown up at just the right time. Today, I get to be the stranger, the one who might make a difference in someone's life. I can be the person who lets someone who is discouraged regain a little faith in mankind. That is the gift I received from strangers.

4. **HUSBANDS** I had more than my share of husbands, but none of the marriages lasted any length of time. That was probably because I got married for every reason but the appropriate one. Each marriage was to fulfill a specific need; to escape, to find some sort of stability, usually financial, to be normal, or my idea of what normal meant, to play house, to justify having sex, even for respectability. I was slow to learn, but the gift I finally received from my marital experiences is the knowledge that no one else could give me what I needed. All the money in the world wouldn't make me feel secure. I couldn't claim self-respect that belonged to someone else. A piece of paper didn't make what I was doing right. Every time I said those marriage vows without meaning them, it was a lie. There was nothing normal about my motives. I couldn't escape myself. The only way I would ever have a successful marriage would be when I didn't "need" to be married, when I could find a way to fulfill all my needs myself.

5. **FRIENDS** I've known many people whom I called "friend." However, I attracted those who were like me: incapable of making a true commitment. You could only be my friend if you understood that I would be there for you unless it was inconvenient for me. I'm sure there were people in my life who truly cared for me and tried to help me, but I pushed them away because the last thing I wanted to hear was the truth. The gift I received from my friends was the knowledge that I could not accept real friends into my life until I figured out how to become a friend. The least I owe a friend is the truth. Real friends don't judge, but are there in good times and bad, even if it is inconvenient. A friend is one who you should be able to think aloud with, without fear of unsolicited advice. Friendship is an important relationship that shouldn't be taken lightly.

I have given you a partial list of all the gifts I've been given. What does it have to do with karma? Karma is about a progression of motivations. Through each seemingly horrible event that took place in my life, I was put in a position to make choices, was forced to change perspectives, and was given the opportunity to progress as a human being. Isn't that what those who believe in reincarnation say? They believe that each life is a learning process that can help, or hinder, the individual in the next life on a personal journey to some destined end. The problem is that you are not forewarned about which life is your last chance.

I've read that the unexamined life is not worth living. Do you suppose that has something to do with karma? To examine is to test by questioning in order to determine progress, fitness, or knowledge. Therefore, you might consider taking a karma quiz to see where you stand.

Karma Quiz

If you believe there is something to karma, and you wonder where you are on the karmic scale, try this twenty-question quiz. Choose the answers that most closely tell your story. There are no right or wrong answers, only the truth. This quiz is designed to be thought-provoking, and is for your eyes only, so you can be brutally honest. See the results at the end of the quiz to learn your karma level.

1. When you think of the most traumatic experience from your past, you:
   - ❑ A. feel no regret, nor wish to close the door on a learning experience.
   - ❑ B. begin, or continue if you've already begun, to question the choices you've made based on the experience.
   - ❑ C. use the experience not to get on with life.
   - ❑ D. feel the same today as you did in the past.

2. When another person with a problem seeks your advice, you:
   - ❑ A. listen and share your experience, strength, and hope.

- ❑ B. give them an honest answer, but wonder if you could do what you suggested.
- ❑ C. help the person and believe he or she owes you.
- ❑ D. feel the person is inept or stupid, and that you deal with bigger problems every day.

3. If a person you care for chooses a lifestyle with which you disagree, you would:
   - ❑ A. still feel the same toward the person.
   - ❑ B. feel compelled to share your fears, and distance yourself emotionally.
   - ❑ C. tell the person what you believe he or she wants to hear so you can be the "good" friend.
   - ❑ D. give the person your sage advice and denounce him or her if he or she doesn't have the sense to follow directions.

4. After you've had a serious disagreement with a family member or close friend, you:
   - ❑ A. consider your part in the situation, and make amends promptly if needed.
   - ❑ B. want to make things right, but fear of confrontation holds you back.
   - ❑ C. hold on to your resentment to be pulled out and used at a later date.
   - ❑ D. blame the other person completely, and cut him or her out of your life until he or she comes crawling back.

5. Aware that you've made a mistake that hurt someone else, you would:
   - ❏ A. apologize and do whatever you could to make it right.
   - ❏ B. avoid contact with that person because seeing him or her reminds you of what you did.
   - ❏ C. apologize profusely, but think the person got what he or she deserved.
   - ❏ D. convince yourself it was no big deal; the person simply overreacted.

6. If you loaned a friend $100.00, and you discovered he or she could not repay you, you would:
   - ❏ A. tell the person it is only money, that he or she can repay you later if possible, and let it go.
   - ❏ B. tell the friend not to worry about it, but you can't forget it.
   - ❏ C. remind your friend he or she owes you at every opportunity.
   - ❏ D. consider the person a deadbeat and threaten to sue.

7. If you realized you were participating in an unhealthy relationship, you would:
   - ❏ A. share honestly about your feelings, and remove yourself.
   - ❏ B. stick it out, believing you have the power to change the situation.

❑ C. stay, feel sorry for yourself, and complain to anyone who would listen.

❑ D. stay long enough to make sure the other person suffers sufficiently.

8. You get angry over:
   ❑ A. very little.
   ❑ B. real, or imagined, injustices.
   ❑ C. others not doing what you expect of them.
   ❑ D. people and circumstances that are out of your control.

9. You express your anger by:
   ❑ A. calm confrontation and words.
   ❑ B. swallowing your feelings and avoidance.
   ❑ C. using sarcasm and sniping.
   ❑ D. yelling and name calling.

10. If you had direct knowledge about the abuse of another, you would:
    ❑ A. get involved by informing the proper authorities.
    ❑ B. turn a blind eye for fear of retribution, and hate yourself.
    ❑ C. tell everyone but the proper authorities about the situation and thrive on the attention.
    ❑ D. tell yourself it's none of your business as long as it doesn't affect you directly.

11. When you are asked to volunteer for community projects or other worthy causes, you:
    - ❏ A. consider if it's something you want to do, and act accordingly.
    - ❏ B. immediately start thinking of excuses not to participate.
    - ❏ C. volunteer, then whine about all you had to do.
    - ❏ D. say "no" because your time is valuable. You have things to do, people to see, and places to be.

12. When you encounter homeless people in need, you:
    - ❏ A. help.
    - ❏ B. pretend you don't see them, walk faster, and regret it later.
    - ❏ C. would help, but tell yourself they would probably spend your money inappropriately.
    - ❏ D. look down on them, imagine that they made their bed, now they can lie in it, give them a look of disgust, and walk past.

13. The party is over, you drank too much, and it's time to go home. You:
    - ❏ A. ask for a ride or call a cab.
    - ❏ B. drive home slowly because you don't want anyone to know you drank too much.
    - ❏ C. blame others for serving you too much alcohol and tell yourself if anything happens it will be on their head.
    - ❏ D. drive yourself without a second thought.

14. You've become aware a friend has an addiction problem. You:
    - ❏ A. truthfully share your concern with the friend.
    - ❏ B. anonymously leave a pamphlet about addiction where your friend will find it.
    - ❏ C. take your friend out for drinks and commiserate with him or her about the problems in your lives.
    - ❏ D. help the friend with excuses as long as the person is fulfilling a need in your life.

15. When you are faced with a limitation, you:
    - ❏ A. see it as a challenge.
    - ❏ B. act as if it doesn't matter, but feel resentful.
    - ❏ C. talk about it but don't take action to overcome, or work around the limitation.
    - ❏ D. live in constant frustration and anger.

16. You express sadness by:
    - ❏ A. allowing yourself to feel what you're feeling, when you're feeling it.
    - ❏ B. acting the way you believe you should, and keeping your feelings to yourself.
    - ❏ C. thriving on the drama of your feelings, and squeezing every bit of attention and sympathy you can get out of them.
    - ❏ D. taking a pill, getting drunk, and choosing anger over sadness.

17. When something good happens in your life, you:
    - ❏ A. celebrate.
    - ❏ B. wait for the other shoe to drop.
    - ❏ C. make sure everyone knows, and that everyone understands how hard you worked, how long you had to wait, and all you suffered before it happened.
    - ❏ D. know you deserve it, and more, and lord it over others.

18. When another person gets what you desired, you:
    - ❏ A. are happy for him or her.
    - ❏ B. want to be happy for the other person, but think it should have been you.
    - ❏ C. do whatever you can to undermine the person or the achievement.
    - ❏ D. wonder what unethical thing the person did to screw you out of what should have been yours.

19. You are happy when:
    - ❏ A. you are alone or with others.
    - ❏ B. you are pleasing others.
    - ❏ C. others understand all that you've endured and overcome.
    - ❏ D. everything, and everybody, is in its place, doing what you want, the way you want it, when you want it.

20. When you look in the mirror, you:
    - ❏ A. see the truth of who you are, and are satisfied.
    - ❏ B. see the truth of who you are, and are not satisfied.
    - ❏ C. see what you want the rest of the world to believe you are.
    - ❏ D. avoid eye contact, focusing on your appearance, not the person behind the eyes.

(Mostly As) Karmic Heart

You are empathetic and nonjudgmental. You have set your feet upon a path of understanding and compassion for others, and for yourself. You listen to your heart and trust your instincts. You and your karma are progressing toward your destiny.

(Mostly Bs) Karma Challenged

Your life lessons are affecting your perception to bring about changes. You are beginning to consider your feelings and question your motives. You have one foot on the path to your destiny, but are hesitant to begin the journey. Fear of the unknown, of not being in control of the outcome, is holding you back.

(Mostly Cs) Karma Martyr

You help when called upon, but afterward feel resentful. You expect payback for services rendered. For you, life is a game of points that can be used for control. Drama is your life's blood. You can't see the path to your destiny because your karma is nailed to a cross.

(Mostly Ds) Karma Interrupted

You have trouble seeing past your own pain and needs. You are harsh in your judgments of others. You do not understand the ripple effect of your choices, and either believe you can control the long-term results of your actions or don't care as long as you are not directly affected. You are struggling in karma quicksand.

If you waited to read the results until after the quiz, you probably took it with honesty and integrity. If you peeked at the results, you are still worried more about image than substance. If you didn't like the results, or didn't agree with them because the author doesn't know or understand you, it was a pointless exercise. If you refused to take the quiz because you consider it trivial, stupid, pointless, and can tell you nothing you don't already know about yourself, there was obviously no reason for you to take it. The whole point of the exercise is to open yourself to where you are, and where you wish to be in terms of karma if, in fact, this is your last, or only, life.

When you spend your time worrying about possible past lives, the next life, or whatever you think happens when you leave this one, it's impossible to be in the moment that is now. For me, karma is about today, this exact moment, and how I am feeling and acting toward myself and others. If my true emotions are not reflected in my actions, I am living against myself, and peace and happiness will elude me.

I believe I am destined to give freely of the gifts I have received in such abundance. I am not to be selective, judgmental, or critical of the people and opportunities that are put in my path, but to believe we are all connected, and that each life has impact.

Can you see the gifts you've been given? Some are wrapped in strange packages. Some you may have to examine more closely than others to understand them. It's all a matter of how willing you are to search, to look beneath the surface. Once discovered, your perceptions will be forever changed. When your perceptions change, so do your feelings—it's like dropping a wrecking ball into the center of that pile of negative emotions and watching them be crushed into oblivion. In that moment, you will be able to match your emotions to your actions and be your authentic self; step off the stage, remove the masks, and let the spotlight shine on you.

Living Inside Out

We all have a unique way of looking at the world, everything and everyone in it, according to where we are in life, and what is important to us at the time. I have looked at the world through many filters and from many angles. Today, I am a writer of inspirational books. I see through a writer's eyes. As I sat in a parking lot in Wickenburg, Arizona, waiting for my friend to return from shopping, my thoughts drifted to this chapter, and what I wished to impart. Red letters flashing across a screen caught my attention. Fascinated, I watched the ads for specials at the store. I had a thought that made me laugh out loud. What if when we were born, the doctors attached a little signboard over our hearts, and whatever we were feeling came up on the screen?

Picture it: you meet a new person, and with each comment made, an emotion lights up on both of your screens. On one hand, there would be no guessing about how the other person felt; on the other hand, you could not hide your true feelings. Anger might show up in red letters, compassion in pink, sadness in blue, serenity in white, envy in green, and joy in gold. At a glance, you would be able to discern the feeling by a color. What do you think of this idea?

Would it be a better way to live? It would certainly simplify the need to play games, save you from getting involved in dishonest relationships, and help you avoid disappointment, even heartache. You would immediately know the futility of placing unrealistic expectations on the other person.

It might be interesting for you to know exactly what another is feeling, but would you want your feelings lit up for everyone to see? It might surprise you to know that I would. It's called "living inside out," and it's how I avoid others expecting me to be anything I am not, feeling anything other than what I'm feeling. With me, what you see is what you get.

The fear of living inside out is that some people will dislike you. They will. It is irrational to believe everyone will like you. However, it is important that you like yourself, and as long as you continue to try to please others, denying the truth of your feelings, your unexpressed emotions will gather into a big ball of clutter that will eventually have a choke hold on your life.

To recognize if your life is in a choke hold, you simply need to investigate. Are you familiar with a feeling of nausea deep in your guts—that feeling one gets when caught in a lie, or doing something untoward? Do you understand the feelings of butterflies fluttering and your heart beating faster when you meet new people or encounter a new circumstance? Do you sometimes experience deep depression or anger for no apparent reason? Do you wonder if you're living on the edge of sanity; that if one more thing happens, you could slip over the edge? The symptoms will vary from individual to individual, but the one thing you must know is that it doesn't matter what things look like on the outside if you know there's something wrong on the inside.

You may think it is an oversimplification to say the solution is to live life inside out. However, it's how I found the answer to ridding myself of the emotional clutter that kept me stuck in an unhappy existence. "What about other people?" you might ask. If you are laying your feelings on the line and others are not, how does that work? As you practice living inside out, you will be amazed at how adept you will become in recognizing those who do not. Besides, when it becomes apparent how you've chosen to live, those who live falsely will avoid you. You will become the mirror they have run from for a lifetime. You will attract those people who live like you, or wish to live like you.

You do not have a little screen over your heart that exposes your emotions in colors and words. What if you did? What would it say? What color would it show? Think about that little screen, the words, the colors, the next time you are in a specific situation or encounter another human being. What would happen if you acted according to your sign, the truth of your feelings? You might be surprised.

When I am successful in staying true to my feelings, I walk away with my self-respect intact, I carry no burden of guilt or shame, my steps are a bit lighter, and I know peace.

When I am not successful, I carry the person or situation away with me, know the weight of guilt and shame, have compromised my self-respect, and suffer the consequences of adding to the big ball of emotional clutter that continues to ruin my life. Knowing that, I'm sure you know the path I've decided to take.

Living inside out is a risk, but believe me when I tell you the results are worth it. In truth, what do you really have to lose? If others don't care about you exactly as you are, if they no longer seek your company, what does it say about the relationship? When I entered into recovery from addiction, do you think those people who were still indulging in their addictions wanted to be around me? Absolutely not! They ran like rats from a sinking ship. I found new friends in recovery, and as time went by, some of those people who ran away returned, seeking what I'd found, and ended up as my dearest friends.

You will know you are practicing the ability to live inside out when what you do matches how you feel. Each time you can accomplish that match, pay attention to how you feel, the results of the encounter. It has been my experience from my own life, and listening to others share their stories, that when you can live inside out, you will like yourself, will change your outlook on others and the world around you, and will be able to clear away all the emotional clutter that is no longer of any productive use. You will finally know peace, happiness, and joy. You will understand that just as you are responsible for your emotional choices, so others are responsible for theirs. You have a choice every day to slap that little screen over your heart, and live accordingly, or not. It's entirely up to you.

TIPS FOR KEEPING IT SIMPLE AND SANE

- The key to keeping life emotionally simple is to take responsibility for your thoughts, actions, and feelings, and to figure out what is holding you back in life and do whatever it takes to fix it.

- You can change unintended consequences by realizing that what you do today can affect you as well as others for years down the road.

- Change what you can, accept what you can't, know you did everything within your power to resolve the issue, and let it go.

- Karma is about motivation. It's not as important what you do, or how you do it, but why you do it.

- When you live inside out, you do not hide your true feelings, but are honest with yourself and those around you; what you do matches how you feel.

Keep It Spiritually Simple

Whatever you do in darkness
will eventually see the light of day.

—Barb Rogers

Spiritual Clutter

One definition of clutter according to *Merriam-Webster's* is "to fill or cover with scattered or disordered things that impede movement or reduce effectiveness." In the case of spirituality, the things that clutter and keep you from moving forward or being effective are questions.

There are so many religions, teachings, opinions, ideas, even books about God, or gods, afterlife, and the dos and don'ts of how to live this one, so how does a person know what to believe? Some people are brought up in a specific religion and follow the guidelines laid out by those who pass on the beliefs that were passed on to them. Others, like myself, must find their own way.

Consider some of the questions that might be cluttering up your spirituality, making you want to throw your hands in the air, and say, "I don't know. I give up. Why bother?"

- Is there a God?
- Does God have a gender, a color?
- If there's a God, why do bad things happen?
- Do we have a soul?
- If we do, does it go on after our body dies?

- Where does it go?
- Is there a heaven and hell?
- Is there one right religion?
- If so, which one is it?
- What is sinful?
- Do we live more than one life?
- Do other species on earth have souls?
- Are there spirits around us?
- If there are spirits around us, why are they here?
- Are there humans that can see them, speak to them?
- Does each person have a purpose?
- If they do, how do I know mine?
- Am I the only one who doesn't know what's going on?

I'm sure there are more questions I haven't considered.

I hope you don't imagine I am capable of answering the questions that might be causing you to feel spiritually paralyzed. I can only answer the questions for myself. I can share my experience, strength, and hope with you, but you must find your own answers.

I had little acquaintance with religion as a child, except when my alcoholic, addicted mother discovered she suffered from a serious lung disease. Suddenly, this little heathen was stuffed into a frilly dress, socks with ruffles, and a hat, and dragged to church on Sundays and Wednesdays. I think it traumatized me. I still have an aversion to ruffles and hats.

Mother chose a very strict religious setting. What I heard was that these people knew exactly what was right or wrong for everyone. However, what I saw was a parent who dressed the part, acted the part on Sundays and Wednesdays, but the rest of the time continued to do what she did before. The only difference was that she attempted to sneak around. It was as if the church people couldn't see her, God wouldn't know.

It was an interesting but confusing time. Mom was taking more pills and drinking less so others wouldn't smell her, having an affair with a young, dreamy evangelist who had come to the church from Alabama to spread the message. I was forced to attend a church camp where I got in so much trouble that Mom had to come and get me. It seemed everything I thought and did was sinful. The whole experience was short-lived, but it was the beginning of unanswered spiritual questions that would clutter up my life for years.

It may not have been a conscious thought, but somewhere along the line I decided from what little I'd heard in church that I was in the fast lane on the way to hell, so I might as well enjoy the ride. After all, as far as I could see, no one could live up to the standards put forth by the church, and even if a person could, why would they choose to live that way?

I became a foxhole prayer, so I guess I believed there was something out there. I only prayed when I was in dire straights—it was kind of like, "God, if you get me out of this mess, I'll never do it again." When I would get into a new scrape after just escaping another, I would try to pray my way out of it too. My personal belief told me it was okay if I got away with it, and wrong if I got caught. Pretty handy, huh?

As my babies struggled to survive, I stood on the other side of the glass barricade, my hand against the cold window, tears streaming down my face, and begged God not to take my children. I promised I would be good. In fact, I attempted to make any kind of deal I could to save their lives. One by one, they died. When my mother shot herself a few months after my youngest son died, I said a halfhearted prayer, but knew it would do no good. She died. For ten years I never uttered another prayer, not even in the worst of times. I'd figured it out. Alcohol and drugs could do for me what God refused to do—give me temporary relief from my thoughts and pain.

Once, after that ten years, I said a prayer, and it haunted me for years and nearly cost me my life. I closed my eyes, and said, "God, if you're there, I need your help. I can't take care of Jon anymore. You'll have to look after him." Jon was my teenaged son, my only living child, and he'd gotten in trouble for stealing a car. Instead of jail, the authorities agreed to allow him to go to a treatment program. He ran away. Not long after I uttered my desperate prayer, he was killed. I felt as if I'd signed his death warrant. Oh yeah, I believed there was a God, and he was big, powerful, mean, and killed children. I had my answers. There was a God, he took everything from me, and I wanted nothing to do with Him. The rest of the questions no longer mattered.

Think of the things you might have prayed about. How did you feel when what you desired didn't happen the way you expected in your time frame? Did you feel like the God you believed in didn't care, or didn't hear your prayers? Have there been times when you've told Him exactly what to do, how to do it, and when, but the results were entirely different than what you were expecting?

It was easier for me to blame God for everything that went wrong in my life than to accept the blame for my part in the situations. I had choices, and I made poor, uninformed ones that brought me to each of my tragedies. God didn't say, "Go ahead, have unprotected sex." Like so many teens, I told myself it wouldn't happen to me. It did. The next choice was to keep the baby. I didn't keep the baby for his sake, but to fulfill my own selfish needs. I needed to be loved, and he loved me. When the doctors told me I was a mess inside, I continued to have babies, always seeking the feeling of being special because I was pregnant, and the unconditional love of a baby. I didn't take good care of myself; the babies were premature, had health problems, and had to struggle for every day of life that they survived.

God didn't show my son how to depend on drugs and alcohol to cope with a life and parent he hadn't chosen. Just as I had learned to cope by watching my mother and others, so did he. God didn't keep my son away from his father so he would feel the need to steal a car to go find him. That was my revenge on his father for getting me pregnant and not loving and taking care of me.

Have you ever been part of a situation in which you blamed God for the outcome? Was one of your big questions, "Why me?" Maybe it's time to take a realistic look at the choices that were made, and who made them. Even when things beyond your control happen that affect your life, there is a choice of how to react. For instance, my mother's suicide had nothing to do with my choices, but I did choose to hang on to the anger, pain, and fear of abandonment as a handy excuse not to commit, not to fully love another.

When I sobered up in a 12-step group, all the original spiritual questions I had returned, and were joined by more. With my new awareness, one new question was, "How would God ever be able to forgive me for the life I've led, the things I've done?" It was soon followed by, "How will I ever be able to forgive myself?" The people in recovery, some of whom had been as bad as I was, others even worse, had found a way. Could it be possible?

In some ways, I think I was lucky I hadn't had years of religious training, because my experience has shown me that it is easier to accept a new idea than to change old teachings that have been imbedded for years. After I got into recovery, I became a spiritual investigator. I read books, listened to others, studied different religions, and still the questions cluttered my mind, keeping me from the life I saw others living. Finally, I sought answers from a woman I'd encountered at some of the meetings. I'd heard her story. She'd lost a child, not to death, but to the State, which deemed her an unfit mother. She'd been at least as awful as I'd been, but according to her, once she found a God of her understanding, everything began to change. I wanted to know how she did that. I caught her after a meeting and inquired of her secret. She said, "All you have to do is care."

Care? What did that mean? She handed me a piece of paper. On it was written:

Connect with a God of your understanding
Ask for help and forgiveness
Take **R**esponsibility
Be willing to make an **E**ffort

She walked away. The first time I read the words, I felt as if someone had punched me in the stomach. I considered wadding the paper up and tossing it in the nearest trash can, but stuck it in my pocket. I shook off the feeling. There was really nothing and no one left to care about. I'd even given up my best friends: alcohol, drugs, and sex. What more did these people expect?

A few days later, as I sorted whites from darks at the laundromat, I found the piece of paper. As I smoothed the crumpled paper and read the words again, I was assailed by the same feeling as before. I read the words over and over, nearly mesmerized by them, hoping they didn't mean what I thought they meant. There was no getting around it—they did. It would take action on my part.

Another question was whether I cared about myself enough to get into action and actually try those things that I heard had worked for others. Suddenly, my mind was flooded with the voices of those who had shared their experience, strength, and hope with me. George said, "You never have to be alone again." Jack said, "You don't have to do it all today. You have a lifetime." Dwight said, "Just because you think something won't work doesn't mean it won't. Look where your best efforts have gotten you." Sharon said, "You only have to do one thing differently, for one day, to bring about change." Neva said, "You will experiment with insanity and death before you will experiment with spirituality." More voices, more messages, continued late into the night.

Have you heard the voices? What were they saying? What did you do with the messages? Did you push them away, try to drown them out with other thoughts, numb them with chemicals, convince yourself things were okay even if deep inside you knew they weren't, for fear of change, of putting your faith in something you can neither see nor touch? It's a big deal, connecting with a God of your understanding; your understanding of life as you know it will be forever changed.

When the questioning put me on the edge, about to fall back into my addiction, I sought out the woman who gave me the piece of paper. She said, "What you need to do is move God from your head to your heart, to understand the difference between believing and real faith."

When I asked her how I could accomplish this, she was thoughtful for a moment, then said, "Imagine that a man stretched a tightrope across Niagara Falls. Every day you walked to the falls and watched him as he balanced a wheelbarrow on the tightrope and successfully pushed it across to the other side. After days of watching him perform this feat, you would certainly believe he could do it, wouldn't you?"

I nodded, fascinated, and waited for her to continue.

"Faith is when you are willing to get in the wheelbarrow," she said, and walked away.

Awakening

After slumber, you open your eyes and focus. You yawn, drawing in great gulps of life-sustaining oxygen. You stretch to loosen the muscles of the body in preparation for movement. Your mind becomes conscious, throwing off the last vestiges of dreamtime. You have awakened.

Is a spiritual awakening really that different? After a metaphorical slumber, you open your heart and soul, and seek clarity. You draw in the life-giving power of a God of your understanding. You stretch that spiritual muscle in prayer in readiness for the day ahead. You become conscious of the reality that is your life, put aside any self-deception, and get into action.

Were you expecting a burning bush, a bright ray of light from the sky, or the appearance of a spirit? It would certainly be easier to recognize and accept if it happened that way. However, through my personal experience and the stories others have shared with me about their spiritual awakenings, I would say those things would be the exception rather than the rule.

I'm not sure that my soul was in a metaphorical slumber. I think it was closer to a coma. There were no signs of activity. With one quick movement and a few words, I was jerked out of that coma. I call it my moment of surrender.

All my life, I'd been a survivor. The word "surrender" was not in my vocabulary. It meant giving up, relinquishing power, yielding, and I believed if I ever did that, I would surely die.

Even as a child, I fought compliance and surrender. I can remember sitting at the table before bedtime, a glass of tepid milk in front of me, so exhausted I could barely hold my head up, unable to surrender to the demands of my stepfather. "All you have to do is drink it, and you can get up," he would say over and over. I hated milk. It made me sick. Eventually, he would put it in the refrigerator and send me to bed, but I knew I would be facing the same glass, the same struggle, the next morning.

I remember telling myself that when I grew up and got away from that house, no one was ever going to make me do anything I didn't want to again. When I was in charge, things would be different. They were different all right . . . but not any better. I took my defiant attitude into jobs, relationships, and every other facet of my life. Maybe that's why I lost so many jobs, many of which I left before they fired me to save my precious pride, failed at one relationship after another, and dwelled in misery and frustration. But, I had the power; I was in charge. At the time, that was all-important.

I surrendered to the fact that I suffered from addictions and that I needed help. I found the help in 12-step meetings with others like me. Problem solved? Not quite. In these steps, the people in the meetings kept referring to a God "of my understanding." They didn't want to know what I understood about God. With all the resentment I had, the deepest was toward God. After all, He was the one who gave me the life I'd lived, had taken everything and everyone away from me. It was okay, though—I could stay because the steps were only "suggested," and I was different from the rest of the people. I didn't need a God in my life.

Time passed; days turned into weeks, then months, and then years. Physically, I was in recovery. Mentally and emotionally, I was confused. Spiritually, I was stunted. I had a place to live, such as it was, an old car that ran part of the time, a job, enough to eat, and an old dog who loved me in spite of myself. What I didn't have was peace. Others, many of whom had come into the meetings after me, had found a way to peace. I wanted to know what it felt like. But my mind whirled on, my emotions continued to choke me, and I flatly refused to think it had anything to do with my lack of spirituality.

Have you ever felt that way? Have you been in a position when things are pretty good in your life, your needs are met, but it feels like something is missing? Do you go to bed exhausted, but can't seem to shut your mind down, to experience that completely rested feeling that carries you into the next day? Are you confused? Do you wonder what it takes to find clarity and peace?

I began to wonder why I wasn't "getting it" and others were. I was running around acting as if everything was fine, as if I was okay, but inside lived a boiling fury that threatened to spill over at the first sign of adversity. As life has a way of doing, it handed me the perfect excuse to return to my addiction, to the self-destructive lifestyle I'd known for so long. The death of someone I'd come to care for was imminent. Fear of loss was always my trigger to self-destruct.

The brain is an amazing organ. It can hold words and ideas from an entire lifetime that you can tap into when the need arises. At times, it might have felt as if you weren't listening or paying attention, but somehow the words seeped in and stuck.

I think that must have been what happened to me. When others in the meetings shared about their spirituality, I shut out their words, did not hear them. However, when the moment of truth occurred, the voices, the words of those who were traveling the path I said I wanted to travel flooded my mind and saved my life. I fell to my knees, begged for help, and surrendered to a God of which I had absolutely no understanding.

I guess I didn't need to understand because this God, whom many called a "Higher Power," knew exactly what I needed. He didn't drop a bag of money at my feet, magically transport me to a better place to live, or fix my car. He didn't bring back those I'd lost or promise that I wouldn't lose others. He gave me what I call the "knowing." In that instant, I knew that everything would be okay, that I would never be alone again, and that no matter what happened from that moment on, I wanted to hang on to that feeling. It was better than any high I'd ever known. For the first time in my life, I knew peace.

I'd always associated the idea of surrender with a loss of personal power, but that day I felt myself empowered. It was no longer me alone, fighting everyone and everything. The fight was over. I surrendered. It was time to get up, heal, and get on with my life.

Since I am a great believer in the one-day-at-a-time concept, even though I had no real understanding of this Higher Power, I knew that if it works today, it will work tomorrow. Therefore, each day I get to have a spiritual awakening. It's simply a matter of rising, kneeling, surrendering, and then living my life to the best of my ability.

From the first moment my knees hit the floor, and I surrendered to a Higher Power I choose to call God, everything in my life changed. Fear was replaced with faith. Dread became excitement. Judgment turned to tolerance, hate to love, and selfishness to gratitude. My circumstances hadn't changed, but my perception of myself, others, and the world around me was forever altered. For the first time in my life I felt there was a purpose for me, that I was going somewhere. I didn't know where, but believed I would be shown the way.

For me, that's the definition of peace. It is knowing that no matter what happens, I am not alone, and everything will ultimately be for my best. I got the very thing I most desired, peace, when I became willing to give up, to say, "I surrender." I'd had a spiritual awakening, and would continue to do so.

If you are wondering how you live life after a spiritual awakening, that will be covered in the knowing that no matter what happens, you are not alone and that everything happens for the best. Believe me when I tell you there probably wasn't another human being more clueless than I about how to live a decent, productive life, and I figured it out—with a great deal of help from others and a lot of divine intervention.

God has great timing and knows what I need when I need it, so as long as I "awaken" each morning and hold tight to my faith throughout the day, everything else simply falls in place. It's like that song "Don't Worry, Be Happy."

As a human being, I don't think it's possible for me to understand God. That's all right, though, because I don't, for example, understand how airplanes fly, but I still get on them. I have faith that whoever does understand these things will keep me safe. The same applies to my soul. The One who understands will get me where I'm headed safely. If I believe that, what is there left to worry about? When I stop worrying, stressing, and trying to make things happen the way I think they should when I want them to, I can be happy and know peace.

Do you live with worry and frustration about things over which you have no control? Are you unhappy with a life that is not what you expected? Do you wonder if there shouldn't be more to life than there has been so far? Are you constantly plagued by questions for which there are no answers? Do you seek clarity and peace of mind?

If you have entertained any, or all, of the questions above, then it's time to consider the "big" question. If you really want the answers, what are you willing to do? Give up? Surrender to a power greater than yourself? Have a spiritual awakening? Live the life you were meant to live? It's your choice.

Wandering Spirit

If your connection to a God of your understanding has been made, whether it's through religion, a recovery program, or a personal experience, it's time to consider what that means to your everyday life. Faith without action is like being dropped into the middle of a forest without a map and compass. You may wander around in the hope of finding your way, but still suffer from frustration, confusion, impatience, and anger.

I know how that feels because I was stuck in that forest for many years. Every time I struck out on my own, I ended up in a worse place than where I began. I finally discovered the map and compass I needed through a 12-step program of recovery. By then, I was ready to try anything. Through the steps I discovered the following.

STEP 1: I needed to stand still, survey the situation through realistic eyes, and acknowledge just how deep I was in my problem.

STEP 2: I needed directions and a guide.

STEP 3: I needed to trust that the guide knew the way.

STEPS 4 & 5: I would have to work at clearing the way.

STEPS 6 & 7: I allowed my guide to help me remove those obstacles that were too much for me to move alone.

STEPS 8 & 9: I needed to continue putting one foot in front of the other and to hold on to my determination to do whatever it took not to turn back.

STEP 10: I resolved never to enter the forest again without my map, compass, and guide.

STEP 11: I understood that the guide who helped me find my way out of the forest and the feelings would continue to guide me as long as I stayed connected.

STEP 12: I needed to be a signpost for others who might be lost, and to share my map, compass, and guide.

The other thing I discovered was that the forest is still there, will be there until the end of my days, waiting patiently for my return. I may have to walk past the forest every day, but I have the tools needed to keep me from getting swallowed up in it again.

You might wonder why a person would reenter a place like that. It was all I'd known for most of my life. I knew what to expect, even if it wasn't pleasant. There is some comfort in knowing what to expect. Staying lost kept me from having to face my fear of the unknown, the questions about what was outside of my comfort zone. It would be a whole new world, new people, new experiences, and no forest in which to hide.

The trees of each forest may be different, representing distinctive problems, but that desperate feeling of being lost is the same. Is there a forest in your life? Have you been wandering without direction, without a guide? Wouldn't it be easy if you could be like Dorothy in the *Wizard of Oz* and simply click your heels together three times, and say, "There's no place like home," with each click? In many ways, it is that easy. Like Dorothy, you have always had the power to get home, but the clicks will be prayers.

Once you've made that connection, have gone home, what then? Are you ready for the new, the unexpected, with no place left to hide? Are you ready to give up your wandering ways for some real direction and guidance? How will you keep from running back into the forest, that old comfort zone?

Using the Seven Deadly Sins for Guidance

It was not easy for me to figure out those things that worked for me, but as I explored new ideas, by opening myself with prayers to a God of my understanding, listening to others who had already traveled the path I desired, and reading books, I was amazed by the glut of information I discovered. I tried many things, some that worked, some that didn't.

One of the not so secret tools is awareness of the seven deadly sins: sloth, pride, greed, lust, envy, gluttony, and wrath. Why are they deadly? Death means to cease to exist, and when I am practicing any of the seven deadly sins, it kills me spiritually. Let me explain by sharing my thoughts on each of the seven deadly sins.

Sloth

When my life improved and things were going well, I got it in my mind that I no longer needed a guide. I became indifferent, apathetic, and spiritless, too lazy to make the connection to a God of my understanding on a daily basis. I was wandering back into the forest. I recognized this through the return of those feelings of frustration, confusion, impatience, and anger. The solution was to begin again, and get into action. I had the tools as long as I wasn't too lazy to use them.

Pride

When false pride takes over, it shows itself by my not believing that I *know* some answers, but that I *am* the answer. In my arrogance, I tell myself that I am one of the chosen people who walk hand in hand with God, and that my way is the only way. If what I did worked for me, then there was something wrong with you if it didn't work for you. It is vanity in its highest form. I might as well be saying, "Look at me. See how I've overcome. You should strive to be like me."

Pride is a heavy burden to carry. While carrying the burden of being a demigod, there will be great disappointment because situations and other people don't live up to those all-important standards. Neither did I. Being prideful is like lying to yourself, then spreading the lie to others. The truth is, left to my own devices, I couldn't cut it; couldn't find my way out of the bathroom. I begged for a guide, for directions, and for the privilege of making my own choices.

The solution was to never forget where I started, why I started, and who helped me, and to never take those things for granted. The way to avoid pride is to hold on to an attitude of gratitude every day. There is always something for which to be grateful if we are willing to acknowledge it.

Greed

Greed is based in fear; fear that there will never be enough. When I believe that anything outside of myself can bring me peace, happiness, and a feeling of security, there will never be enough. Greed denies spirituality. If I am truly spiritual, I know that the answer lies within.

If money and possessions brought happiness and peace, it stands to reason that the wealthy would not fall into addictions, commit crimes, or commit suicide. However, that is not the case. Life is in a constant state of fluctuation. Some changes are made through choice, but many are not. A sudden health problem, the loss of loved ones, possessions, money, jobs, even mental abilities, are indicators there is no security in life, except for the security that lives in the hearts and minds of the spiritual. They know the secret to happiness, peace, and a feeling of security.

What is the great secret they know that took me such a long time to figure out? It's that when I'm connected every day, in all things, to a God of my understanding, there is always enough because I am where I'm supposed to be, doing what I'm supposed to do, with the people I need to be with at that moment. When I live in the truth of who I am, never compromising myself and my God, even when bad things happen I know it's okay to be happy, know peace, and feel secure. I am never alone, and my guide will always show me the way.

Greed and spirituality cannot abide side by side. It's not the things that show greed, but the importance and expectations put on things that are the problem. Eventually, all the things, including the physical body, will pass away. What will be left? It can be called the soul, spirit, ghost, essence of the true self, even the God self, but it doesn't matter what it's called, it's the belief that a part of me endures. If that part of me endures, why would it not be of uppermost concern?

Lust

To know lust is to feel disconnected, unloved, untouched. It shows itself by a constant sexual obsession. The closest the lustful feel to love is during the sexual encounter. However, it's not really love, it's simply sex. Sex can be an expression of love, but love is not sex.

The touch of all the physical hands on earth cannot give me the feelings I desire. That emotion comes through the invisible hand of the God of my understanding, who wraps me in His warm embrace and lets me know that, no matter what, everything will be okay. With that feeling comes the knowledge that I'm connected to all of humanity simply because I'm here. It lets me know that I am loved unconditionally, in a way that no other human being can love me. I have been touched by the hand of God, and there is no other touch that can compare.

I will not recognize the love of another until I love myself. I will not love myself until I know the love of the unseen. I will not share love until I know love. Anyone with the right equipment can have sex, but to love and be loved is a special gift.

In *Sand and Foam*, Kahlil Gibran wrote, "Strange, the desire for certain pleasures is part of my pain." With lust, the pain comes from continuing to try to capture a fleeting feeling.

Envy

Envy obliterates uniqueness, and reduces opportunities and abilities. Every time I am envious of you, of others, for what you have, can do, advantages you've had that I didn't, I give up a bit of my uniqueness by comparison. As long as I focus on you and your life, the many opportunities that are mine alone will elude me. I will not fulfill the potential of my abilities because I cannot see them.

When I live in envy, it's to avoid the responsibility that is my own life, my own set of circumstances. When I attempt to usurp what does not belong to me, whether it be a position, the affection of another person, a possession, or respect, it will not fill my cup.

I believe there is purpose for each life, or we wouldn't be here. There will be ups and downs, life lessons and reasons for them, and I need to pay attention to my own path. If I keep jumping on yours, trying to take it over, or place hurdles in your way because of my envy, I cannot reach my destiny.

If you believe in a God of your understanding, and you suffer from envy, it's like telling your God that He didn't get it right.

Maybe you think you should have been born to a different family, had more advantages, or had less strife. Do you think this God knows less than you? If that's the case, why bother with a God at all?

Gluttony

Gluttony is often associated with food, but it means so much more. It's about excess in many areas of life. I know a lot about gluttony because I did everything in excess at one time or another . . . except eat. That was because food tended to take the edge off my buzz when I overindulged in alcohol, which was quite often. And, when I threw up, I preferred liquids.

Gluttony is the disease of the cluttered, disquieted, unfocused mind. Whatever I did to excess was used to escape and quiet the thoughts that plagued my mind. It's a fix, but like all fixes, it didn't last long before I needed another one. As time went on, I would need more and more extremes to get the same feeling. The time between the fix got shorter and the effects diminished until it became my obsession.

An obsession is "a persistent disturbing preoccupation with an often unreasonable idea or feeling," according to *Merriam-Webster's*. If you wonder if you can be a spiritual person and still indulge an obsession, I'll share with you what was told to me: "You can only serve one God."

If you wonder if something is an obsession, there is an easy way to figure it out: try not to do it for a period of time, try not to think about doing it, or not doing it, and pay attention to the results. The answer will become clear in a short time. If you find yourself making excuses and justifying continuing the behavior, it's a clear indicator that there is a problem.

Gluttony will leave no room for spirituality. If I want to live a spiritual life, I must become willing to do whatever it takes to rid myself of whatever obsession stands in my way.

Wrath

Let's call it by the name with which we are more familiar. Wrath is rage. It is rage that wants vengeance. Rage is the silent, deadly killer of the spirit. Mine began in childhood, and I nurtured it for years until there was no room left for anything else in my life.

Wrath is the most self-centered of the seven deadly sins, and can actually physically hurt someone, or those around that person. The extent of pain caused is in direct correlation to how long the rage has been held within, and how big it has grown. It's like a growing cancer. Every minute, every hour, every day, every year, it grows and becomes more imbedded in the heart, and eats away at the spirit.

Living in rage is living in self-pity. I had illusions about what my life should be, and imagined that I was denied my dreams through circumstances and people out of my control. It was all about me: what others did or didn't do for me, situations that really had nothing to do with me, and the choices I told myself I was forced to make. I blamed everything and everyone, and refused to take responsibility, and the cancer called rage grew.

To become a spiritual individual, it was necessary to take responsibility for every choice, action, and reaction in my life. I learned that others do not live their lives concerned with mine. They don't do things to me, but for themselves. Most situations are not about me, and are not my business. My business is taking care of me. God does not need me to help Him right wrongs, nor does anyone else. Each person is responsible for their own life and choices . . . and they don't have to affect me.

Releasing every excuse I'd used for self-pity was the treatment for the cancer I call rage. Taking responsibility for my life and living it in a spiritual way was the continued treatment. If I am living in the sight of a God of my understanding, within reach of a mirror, I will not know rage.

Each of the seven deadly sins you allow to influence your life will bring you one step closer to the forest of lost souls. If you suffer from any, or all, of the deadly sins, and you are aware of it, that's the first step to change. The solution is to practice the opposite behavior of whatever sin you are suffering from. To practice, you must be actively engaged.

Since I suffered from envy, among other things, when I became ready to change that, I had to first find a way of understanding the origin. It was self-pity; seeing my glass as half full and everyone else's as overflowing. I wanted what they had, but was not willing to do what they did. It was easier to cry "foul" and tell myself life was unfair.

Once reality hit, I located a person I knew to have a generous soul, who always wished others well. I asked how she accomplished such a feat. She said that when she had an envy problem with another, she prayed for them. Every day, she prayed for the other person to have all those things she desired most in her life.

You will be handed ample opportunities to do things differently. The trick is to recognize the opportunities when they arise and make the most of them. You don't even have to believe it will work; simply try it for a period of time and see what happens.

If you are in doubt about what to do, ask your guide. I've heard it said that you should be careful what you ask for because you might just get it. If you ask for patience, you may be faced with situations that will test your patience. That seems to be the way it works.

Embrace Uncertainty

Life would be a bore if we had foreknowledge of what would happen, and when it would occur. Uncertainty brings with it one of two things: dread or excitement. Those who dread uncertainty will plow through life filled with fear, many times seeking answers in the strangest ways, while those who excitedly anticipate uncertainty will sail through life, welcoming its challenges as opportunities for spiritual growth.

I lived in fear of everything and everyone. Of course, I presented myself as self-assured, outgoing, able to handle anything. However, it was all words and bluster to hide the truth. The truth lived in the shadows of my life. There had been so many surprises and shocks in my life, and I wanted answers. I experimented with drugs that I heard would "expand my mind," sought answers through mediums and psychics, read book after book, and ended up addicted and financially challenged, with even more questions.

I was like Jekyll and Hyde; two totally different personalities sharing the same body. Around others, the tough broad, the party girl, the one tagged "Smiley" who acted as if everything was fine, emerged. The magic potion that turned me into Hyde could be bought in any liquor store or bar. I may not have grown fangs and hairy knuckles, but I became a terror, not only to others, but also to myself. I did horrible things, with no memory of them the following day. Eventually, Hyde took over completely, which intensified the dread of every new day.

If I couldn't black out or pass out, fear brought on the night terrors. For those of you who are not familiar with night terrors, experiencing one is like actually living in one of Stephen King's horror books or movies. I remember once, when I was pregnant with my daughter and off the magic potion, that I awoke in the night and could see my 2-year-old son standing at the end of my bed with blood gushing from his mouth. It was so real; I could hear someone screaming, but didn't realize it was me. Someone in the trailer court called the police—I'm sure they thought I was being murdered. I was only 17 years old, but dread caused by fear brought me to the point of exhaustion on a daily basis.

Have you ever known that feeling of simply being exhausted with life, tired of facing each day, overwhelmed with unanswered questions? Are fear and dread your constant companions? Do you wonder how to move from fear and dread to excitement?

I've heard it said that we are spiritual beings having a physical experience. If that's true, then we are here to experience, to learn all that this life has to offer. If we knew the answers up front, what would be the point? Learning is progression through experience that changes behavior.

Your life here on earth as a school is an interesting concept. It would explain many things. In school you had teachers who attempted to share their wise words, books with a myriad of ideas, tests to see how much you'd learned, and if you did well, you progressed to a higher level until you graduated. That sounds a lot like life.

In school, I was unfocused, uninterested, refused to sit still or listen, and had to retake many tests before I could advance. I questioned absolutely everything from what I was being taught to the qualifications of those attempting to teach me. It all seemed so pointless. I carried that same attitude into life. I dreaded every day I was forced to attend school, and when I got out, dreaded every day I had to face my life. I am not sure it was so much fear of uncertainty or being certain that something bad was always waiting just around the corner that caused my dread, but I know it was fear of how and when it would happen.

Why not give up? I don't know. I thought about it regularly, planned my death in many dramatic ways, and lived with the hope that I would go to sleep and not awaken. For years I told myself I couldn't die because I was the only parent on which my one living child could count. He needed me. I remember after he was killed that I sat on his grave, drunk, raging about how unfair our lives had been, how he hadn't really had a chance in life, and imagined I would take poison and throw myself across his grave and die. I would show the world, make them sit up and take notice, make them sorry for the way they'd treated us. Instead, I passed out and came to hours later with dirt all over my face.

For five more years, I nurtured my rage, which I believed excused my bad behavior. When driving my car, I'd think about running it off a cliff or over a bridge. I considered committing a crime and not giving up so the police would shoot me. I was consumed with death, yet didn't realize I was slowly committing suicide with what I was putting in my body. Obviously I didn't want to die, but I couldn't stand living the way I'd chosen. I was so tired: tired of waking up each morning; tired of terrible, hateful thoughts; tired of living with a black cloud of dread following me everywhere; tired of always feeling tired.

Getting into a recovery program was like going back to school. I've heard it said that a 12-step program is like getting a million dollars worth of information and skills fed to you one nickel at a time. That's pretty much what it was like for me. I was also told that it was a program based in spirituality. I believed I could do it without spirituality, but discovered that, until I found a God of my understanding, I could not move forward.

Have you ever watched the Dr. Phil show on television? When he says, "I want you to get excited about your life," how does it make you feel? Does a knot form inside, do tears well in your eyes because you want to be excited about your life but aren't, or do you get goose bumps because you are? How you react to words can tell you a lot about where you are at the moment and where you wish to be.

Do you ask yourself what there is to get excited about? As odd as it may seem, I know it's embracing uncertainty. Every day is a new opportunity to start over, and I have a choice in everything. When I hit a slump or get a bad attitude, I can start the day over at any time. There is, in fact, always something right around the corner. The excitement comes from each encounter with whatever or whoever might enter my life.

When I stopped believing I was in control, expecting dreadful situations, asking questions for which there were no answers, and began allowing teachers and faith into my life, it became clear.

Earlier in life, when something seemingly bad happened, it would stop me in my tracks. Today, I see those hurdles in my path as a challenge. I stop, ask for guidance from a God of my understanding, listen, and get into action. One of the great challenges I've encountered in the past few years has to do with writing books. Although I began writing because I had a disease that prohibited me from continuing to pursue costume design, doing housework, driving, or do much else, I instantly knew it was what I wanted to do . . . that I could punch away on an old typewriter with no real idea of what it meant to be a writer or sell a book.

Graves' disease was the first challenge in writing. The treatment killed my thyroid. I was left with little energy. I suffered from excruciating headaches that lasted days, sometimes weeks. Every day I awakened with a feeling of sand in my eyes, with skin that itched so badly I could barely stand it, and watched as my hair fell out into the sink. Except for telling me I was looking at a number of years of recovery, and possible eye surgeries, the doctors were of little help. I chose to accept the challenge.

First things first. I needed to understand my disease. I read everything I could get my hands on, talked to those in the know, and questioned the doctors who were caring for me. I accepted the disease by getting over the "Why me?" feeling by asking myself "Why not me?" What made me think I should be exempt where others are not? Stuff happens to everyone.

Every day I prayed, turning my will, my life, and my disease over to a God of my understanding, and had faith that no matter what happened, it would be okay. Even if I died, which I felt like I would some days, I appreciated the opportunity I'd had to know love, forgiveness, and to grow and change into the person I had always wanted to be.

I shaved the sides of my head so I wouldn't look like I had mange, wrapped myself in a sheet so the seams in clothing wouldn't burn my skin, became an eyedrop connoisseur, reserved my energy by not killing myself trying to do things that wouldn't matter if I died anyway, and kept typing until I could do it without looking. I became willing to do whatever it took to recover, and to be a writer.

Have you ever wanted something so bad that you would be willing to do whatever it took to find a way? Think of those times in your life when you've had to overcome challenges. It may have happened in baby steps, may have taken a long time, but how did you feel about yourself when it worked? Did you ask for help through divine intervention? If so, do you believe that made a difference?

My next challenge was rejection. Apparently, I wasn't a very good writer. The options were to give up, keep writing crap, or learn. Just as I had to learn about my disease, many times through trial and error, I had to take criticism of my writing skills and do whatever it took to make them better. Instead of becoming angry at the rejections, I looked at them as a tool I could use to achieve my ultimate goal. It worked. I was published.

Challenge number three was the computer. I'd recovered from the disease, had the eye surgeries, was a published author, but needed to learn to use a computer. Filled with excitement, I went computer shopping. I knew it would make writing so much easier. As I learned to work the new computer, I noticed the headaches returning. Within a short time, I discovered that the matrix on the computer screen was causing the muscles behind my eyes to swell and pinch my optic nerves. I must admit, I was disappointed, even a bit discouraged. The choices were to give up in disgust and tell myself life was unfair, or to be grateful that I could see and still use the old typewriter. I chose the latter.

Have you begun to see how embracing uncertainty, changing your perception of life and situations over which you have no control, can bring about excitement through challenge? Each time you accept a challenge, ask for help, and overcome, you progress, grow, and move forward.

For years, I have placed my faith in a God of my under-standing in all areas of my life, including my writing. He has led me to some unexpected places and some interesting people. Life was good, books were being published, and I was grateful every day for the gift of being able to express myself in the written word. In one moment, that changed.

My little Italian greyhound, Sammi, died unexpectedly from cancer. Are you thinking, "It was just a dog"? She wasn't simply a dog to me. When I'd been so ill with Graves' disease, unable to function in the world, even in my own home, my husband brought her to me as a companion. She helped me stay out of myself, out of the pain, and brought me so much joy. I gave her the love I might have given a child if I'd been capable at the time. When she died, I was devastated.

Suddenly, the worst pain I'd ever known gripped my right side. It didn't go away. When I sat down, it was unbearable. Doctor after doctor ran tests, guessed at what might have happened, but the pain remained. It's hard to live life either standing up or lying down. I stopped driving, I stopped writing. I stopped functioning in the world, in my home, yet again. What to do?

Being a true believer that everything happens for a reason, although it certainly isn't always clear, I accepted the pain and the challenge. Unable to take pain medication because of allergies, left undiagnosed, the only thing I knew to do was pray. My primary doctor, a loving, caring man, sent me to see a friend of his. Apparently, the death of my beloved dog precipitated inside shingles that had gotten into my nerves, which was causing the pain. He said it would either stop on its own, or could last for years.

After I got over being stunned at the diagnosis and prognosis, I told myself it was time to get into action. For me, getting into action always begins with prayer, meditation, and the belief that everything will be okay. Where there is faith, there is always a way. I didn't pray for the pain to be removed, but to understand what it was I needed to do, for those who might help me to be put in my path, and that I might recognize them.

It was time to get on with my life and discover what I was capable of doing rather than the limitations. My husband helped me move the furniture to accommodate the situation. Instead of a desk to write on, the typewriter was moved to a tall table. A half bed became the place from which I could watch television or read. We moved to the bar to eat because I could stand up. I simply had to endure the pain to drive, so I walked more often. It was a challenge, but as long as I adjusted my surroundings to the problem, I could endure the pain. I was absolutely amazed at all the things I could do standing up or lying down.

Have you been tested? Do you understand how capable you truly are? The point isn't whether you are capable or not, but that you can do whatever you need to do and still hold on to your joy, cheerfulness, and continue to see what you have, and not what you lack. A friend once told me that when she prays, she says, "If I can't have what I want, please help me to want what I have."

Eventually, I was led to a very spiritual acupuncturist who helped me with the pain. She said it wasn't simply the pain of loss at and stress of losing Sammi that triggered the shingles inside me, but that when my dog died, I grabbed on to the memory of all the pain I'd suffered through the loss of my children. She said that some believe we carry the pain of loss in the liver section of the body. That certainly was where it hurt. Through discussing past trauma and sticking thin needles here and there in my body, in five sessions the pain was gone. Many others who knew of my situation have since tried acupuncture and found relief. Do you suppose the pain wasn't about me, but that I might have simply been a messenger for another?

Uncertainty is not only about not knowing what is going to happen, but also why things occur. Have you ever thought that perhaps it's not always about you? If you are, as some believe, connected to all of humanity, could it be possible that your path will cross the paths of others, and at times you will be someone's fleshy angel, and at other times a person who crosses your path will be yours?

As I reflect on my past and think of the plans I made that were changed in one moment, by one word or another person, I get chills. How I ended up a writer of inspirational books instead of in prison, committed to an asylum, or dead, amazes me. If you had known me back before I began recovery, you might have given me a two percent chance of making it past age 30, and a zero percent chance of ever knowing what it is to be happy. Yet, here I am this morning, over 60 years old, writing, loving, and happy because I have learned to embrace uncertainty.

Perhaps there was a plan for me of which I was unaware. If that's true, which I believe is the case, then it took every moment, every person who crossed my path, every bit of pain I felt, all those situations that were out of my control, to bring me to this exact point in time to do what it is I'm doing. When I look at my life from that perspective, it enables me to know that nothing is bad if it can be used as a tool to help myself, and possibly help others.

The excitement of embracing uncertainty can only come from one place: faith. Faith is personal. I can talk and write about those things I believe or don't believe. Others share their experience and thoughts in many ways. Faith, however, is a feeling for which there is no explanation. It's a feeling, a knowing, that lives in the deepest part of the human spirit. How do you know if you have faith? You know because it is as much a part of your body as your limbs, your brain, your heart. When you have faith, you embrace uncertainty. When you have faith, you live in the truth of who you are when you're alone, or with others. When you have faith, it's easy to get excited about your life, live in the moment, and know that no matter what happens, it will be okay.

Faith is not ambiguous. Either you have it or you don't, and only you know.

Spiritual "Tells"

A "tell" is the physical manifestation of the truth. A poker player uses tells to determine if his opponent is bluffing. He watches for particular mannerisms, and associates them with winning and losing. The opponent might raise his eyebrows when he has a winning hand or clear his throat when the cards don't fall his way.

Therapists use tells to help them understand what is really going on with a client, aside from what the client is saying. If a client is pretending to be open and honest, but sits in the chair with his arms folded across his chest, the therapist might surmise he is guarding a secret or holding back. The therapist will insert specific words in his dialogue and watch for a physical response. Did the gaze shift to the right or left? Did the client run his hands through his hair? Did he purse his lips, tap his fingers, or swing his leg? These are tells that are used to guide therapy in the right direction.

A jury consultant is hired to observe potential jurors for an attorney during the selection process of a trial. When the consultant observes, what is it you think he's watching?

He's watching for any tells that might inform him a juror might or might not be sympathetic to either side of the trial for which he's hired. It could be a look, the way a juror sits in the chair, if a juror hesitates before answering a key question, even the quality of the juror's jewelry. Could a wealthy woman relate to a poor female client who has been indicted for stealing?

When I work with others in crisis, I watch and listen for tells. When I hear words such as "should" and "can't," it tells me the person feels powerless. "Yes, but" means the person is not willing to change the problem. Eye movement tells me a lot. When a person looks up, it means they are rethinking, and when they look down, it means they are refeeling. Looking at the hands, feet, or tabletop indicates avoidance. I recall one woman, who, as I realized after having spent time with her, played with or pulled on her bottom lip every time she lied.

Most people have tells of which they are unaware. Pay attention to yourself. Do you pull on your earlobe when you tell a lie? Do you scratch at your chin when you are uncomfortable? Do you twirl a strand of hair when you are into avoidance? What words do you use when you're confronted with a situation you want to talk about, but don't really want to change?

You would be amazed at how often you subconsciously use tells in different relationships. Think back. Did you ever have a suspicious feeling when you first met someone? There were no facts to back it up, it wasn't about what the person said, but you simply knew, and were right. You picked up on a tell. It occurs more often than you think.

Spiritual tells work much the same way. Why is it important to understand tells in yourself and in others? It's important because it reveals whether you are living in the truth of your beliefs, or living in conflict between who you are and whom you profess to be. It's important to understand tells in others because if you decide to seek council from another, you need to know that person understands the issue better than you. Why would you listen to someone who is worse off than you?

The first thing to consider is what it is you believe. Be careful when you decide on morals, ethics, appropriate behavior, and what is right or wrong for others. If it wrong for them, it must certainly be wrong for you. It's simply too easy to focus outside yourself, to put expectations, many times unrealistic expectations, on others when you don't live up to them yourself. Sooner or later, others will notice the tells that show you for who you really are.

If you wonder about your spiritual tells, consider these questions:

1. Do you compare yourself to others and find something to criticize about them so you feel better about yourself?

2. Do you tend to condemn others, and situations, without really knowing the whole story?

3. Do you complain about others, and circumstances, to bring attention to yourself?

4. Do you have one set of morals and values for others, but can justify not living up to them yourself?

5. Do you feel you have the right to put expectations on others?

6. When things don't work out the way you expect them to, how do you react?

Children have a knack for picking up on tells. I think it's because their minds are not as cluttered. Before my oldest son died, he was the mirror into which I needed to look. I can still see him, his big blue trusting eyes, looking up at me and saying, "But, Mom, you said everyone deserves a second chance." I did say that, but looking back, I realize I was talking about myself. I deserved a second chance, but was I willing to give it to others? Was I willing to allow his friendship with a troubled young boy who had acted inappropriately in my house, who had made his apology and asked to return?

"But, Mom," he said, "you said to stand up for what I believe." I didn't mean for him to stand up against a teacher, a coach, or a principal. It made things terribly inconvenient for me. For instance, when he was in Little League, and one of the better players, at one game he walked off the field and refused to return. The coach summoned me to speak to him. When I asked him why he had walked off, he said, "It's not fair. The coach is supposed to play everyone. He won't let Timmy play." His eyes shifted to the bench where a thin boy with glasses sat alone.

I loved sitting in the stands, filled with pride at how well my son played ball. I enjoyed the accolades from the other parents. The coach said that if he didn't play, he would be off the team. I tried to convince him to return to the game, and said we would deal with the Timmy problem later.

I should have known from the stubborn set of his jaw and the look in his eyes that he wasn't going anywhere. His response to the coach was, "If Timmy doesn't play, I don't play." Things worked out well, and both boys got to play, but I was left with the knowledge that a preteen child had more integrity than I did.

In my son's few short years of life, he taught me so much. It took some time for me to get things through my thick head, so filled with clutter from the past, but I finally began to understand. Children truly do live in the moment and have a clarity that is only experienced through an uncluttered spirit. I often wondered if he came here to teach me and stayed only as long as was needed. The last couple of years before he died, I'd even begun to pollute him, his purity of spirit, his wonderful sense of right and wrong, and his beliefs. Maybe he needed to go before he turned into me.

The Four "Cs"

I was the epitome of a person who presented herself well, talked a good story, but lived in the opposite way. As soon as someone began to spot my tells and call me out on them, I moved on to someone else I could fool . . . at least for a while. It's impossible to develop intimate, long-term relationships while living on the run. It didn't matter where I went, because there I was, and as long as I refused to look at my tells, to have the courage to be the person I wanted people to believe I was, I would be destined to live in fear of being found out and in unhappiness caused by living in constant conflict.

What are these spiritual tells? There are four "Cs" that can reveal a discontented life: competing, criticizing, condemning, and complaining. When any, or all, of them begin to surface, watch out. To identify them, you simply pay attention to the true thoughts and feelings you're experiencing.

To compete is to compare yourself with others. It's a martyr thing. You might have thoughts like, "Well, sure, if I had his life/money/wife/health/kids, I'd be happy too. If I hadn't had to struggle for every little thing in life, I could run around with a smile on my face like his." Feelings of jealousy, envy, and resentment could ensue. Do you think those feelings are affecting the other person? No, the one affected would be you, pacing the floor with a headache, scowling at those around you, and living in the "if only's," e.g., "If only my life had been better, I would be better."

That's not true. Your life would be different, but not necessarily better. For one thing, you're only seeing the other person's life from the outside. You have no idea what is going on inside them, where they have been in life, what they have experienced. You know how you present yourself to the world, how you hide your true thoughts and feelings. What if the other person is doing the same thing?

When an individual is spiritually fit, he or she knows that life is not a competition. The word "competition" brings with it words like "winners" and "losers." What makes a person a winner? Pick someone you admire, whom you see as a winner, and write down the top five reasons for that belief. I will share with you what I wrote about the person I most admire.

1. You don't have to earn his love, his kindness, or his compassion.

2. If he were starving, he would give you his food if he thought you were in greater need.

3. He lives in his truth, without feeling a need to explain or justify who he is or the choices he makes.

4. He forgives himself and others for not being perfect.

5. It's not necessary for him to understand or agree, but he would fight for your right to pursue your dreams.

Is he a saint? Is he perfect? Is he Superman? No, he's just a man living life to the best of his ability. Since I've known him for forty years, and have been married to him for twenty-one of them, I know there is no pretense, no guile, no jealousy or envy in him. He is exactly who he appears to be.

What did you write down about the person you admire? If it had anything to do with money, possessions, a career, or appearances, you've missed the point. Those things are not who the person is, but what they do, what they own, what they look like. Who a person really is, is what they take with them wherever they go, whatever they're doing, no matter whom they are with. That's whom I strive to be on a daily basis.

If you're criticizing others, it serves one of two purposes. It's either to keep the focus off of you or to attempt to tear the person down to what you consider your level so you don't have to feel bad about who you are. I can recall a time in my life when I was critical of everyone. I could always find someone to look down on so I could tell myself at least I wasn't that bad, that stupid, that ugly, that perverted, or that addicted. Out loud, I'd say, "Did you see her? She's a mess. And what was she thinking with that hairdo, that outfit? Could she have put any more makeup on? She's such a slut." *Hello*! I may have been pointing one finger at her, but there were three fingers pointing back at me. However, if I could keep you looking at her, thinking about her, talking about her, maybe you wouldn't notice me.

Once, when reading a list of questions about addiction, I had to laugh out loud. One of the questions was, "Did you run with lower companions?" The truth was, I was the lower companion, but because I criticized others to keep the focus off me, it would take you a while to notice. By then, I'd probably moved on to another unsuspecting individual.

Today, I understand that we are all unique, interesting, complex individuals, who bring with us all of our life experiences. The Hawaiian people I met while traveling there for a writers' retreat and conference helped me to understand that when they told me that their belief is when you meet someone new, all your ancestors, and theirs, are there too. For me, it means we bring all the teachings, the beliefs, the changes, and the growth of all we've encountered to that meeting, as does the other person. What a great concept. We are, after all, an accumulation of all we've been, all we've done, and all we've learned up to this moment in time. We cannot be any more, or any less, than what we are. The question becomes, who are we to criticize another?

When the critical thoughts come, and you hear the words leave your lips, a red flag should go up immediately. What do those other three fingers pointing back at you mean? What need are you fulfilling by criticizing another? What is not right within you to drive you to this desperate act? It is a desperate, mean-spirited effort, designed to inflict pain.

If you're really good at criticizing others and you find there is a payoff, such as being the person in the know, sought out for your ability to gossip, thought wise for your perception of others, you can become the judge and jury. You're then in a position to condemn.

Condemnation is born of ignorance. I often wonder if a person would be so quick to condemn if they were forced into close quarters with the one they are condemning and had the opportunity to truly know the person. It's too easy to sit back, puff yourself up, and condemn another when you haven't walked in their shoes. Given the same set of circumstances, you don't know what you would have done differently.

Who is deserving of our compassion? If you are spiritually fit, you know the answer. You may hate what someone does, but not the person. We can separate the action from the person. You might be thinking, what about when someone kills a person you love? When my teenage son was killed, it was the greatest devastation of my life. He was my only living child, the one constant in my life, and the only thing decent about my life up to that point.

I wasn't religious, didn't even consider myself spiritual, but even as a drunk and everything that went along with it, I did feel compassion for the young man who killed my son. It was an accident. I wrote him a letter because I thought if it had happened to me, I would have so many questions about the person I killed. I told him about my son, about our life, and let him know I didn't blame him. After all, my son was gone; there was no reason for another young man's life to be destroyed.

I learned about compassion from the uncompassionate. Much of my life I'd been gossiped about, condemned, and ostracized, as had my son, because of my actions. I wasn't a bad person—I simply made some poor choices, and did some bad things. I have learned to have compassion for myself by knowing I did the best I could at the time, with what I had to work with. It wasn't much, but it was all I had.

Even when I hear of someone committing a horrendous act, I hate what they did, but must wonder what in the world happened to that person to drive them to do it. Having spent time with people who have been imprisoned, and knowing it was only through grace that I didn't end up there, I know there are worse things than being put to death. It is living with the truth of your actions, taking responsibility for your choices. I believe that sooner or later, everyone will be accountable for every action they take.

The fourth spiritual tell is to complain. If you want to know what you complain about and how often, try carrying a small notebook and pen with you for one day. Each time you complain, make a note. At the end of the day, read what you've written and think about it. Ask yourself how important each complaint was. If it was important, what action did you take to make it better? If it wasn't important, why were you willing to give up one moment of your life, your peace, to worry about it?

The following day, take the notebook with you again, but this time, each time you write down a complaint, write down something for which you are grateful next to it. In the book, you might have written something like:

December 21st

9:00 a.m., on the way to work
    Complaint: *The weather is freezing. I'm cold.*
    Gratitude: *I have a warm coat, boots, and gloves.*

Noon, lunch with coworkers
    Complaint: *They don't pay me enough to do this job.*
    Gratitude: *I have a good education. I could get another job.*

6:00 p.m., watching the news
    Complaint: *There's nothing but crap on the tube.*
    Gratitude: *I have the ability, the choice, to turn it off and do something else.*

10:00 p.m., bedtime
    Complaint: *My back hurts.*
    Gratitude: *I can afford my medication.*

Complaining is for those who wish to be noticed, who want to make others see them as involved, important, and smart. It is an ego thing. It's the same as saying "see me, hear me, know I'm upset, and that it's important."

If you are content with yourself and your life, you know the answer to a complaint is to take action. If you are unhappy with politics, vote, pass out fliers, or run for office. All the complaining in the world won't change things. If you have a health issue, find answers, try things, even alternative forms of healing, and know you are doing everything you can on your own behalf. Don't dwell on what you are not capable of, but what you can do. Taking action, and knowing there is always something to be grateful for, even if it's only the ability to breathe in and out, is the answer.

Someone once told me we are not given more than we can handle. I remember thinking that whatever was out there in charge of things had mistaken me for someone much larger. I survived, I learned, and eventually, I began to live. If one thing had happened differently, I would not be the person I am today, doing what I'm doing. Through that particular life lesson, I've come to believe that I am on a life path, and that there is a reason for everything.

If you believe one thing happened for a reason in your life, then you must accept that all things happen for a reason. You don't get to pick and choose. For me, it's as simple as spirituality. Either you believe in a higher guidance, or you don't. If you are thinking that you are an agnostic, that you just don't know, perhaps you need to find out. Otherwise, your life will be cluttered by constant questioning.

There are those who would say there is no proof of the existence of a Higher Power. I would say to them that I am living proof. I could not have come from where I did, lived through all I've lived through, and come out on the other side a happy, healthy, content human being without divine intervention. Believe me when I tell you that no one is more amazed than I.

The change in my life began the day I dropped to my knees and begged for help from something I didn't even believe was there. That one moment of desperation was the defining moment that brought me to the life I know today. It wasn't about getting a second chance in life. It was my only chance to actually live life.

If you are interested in simplifying your spiritual life, become an explorer. You won't be searching outside yourself, but in the dark corners of your soul, your thoughts, and your actions. That's where you will find the answers. To unclutter, you will be cleaning out and exposing to the light all those old cobweb-filled areas that you've hidden from the world. It's much like cleaning out your living space. You know that wonderful feeling you get when it's done, when everything is in its place and shiny, when you can let out that deep sigh of relief? Uncluttering your soul gives you the same feeling.

To maintain that feeling, stay aware. Watch out for the four "Cs": compete, criticize, condemn, and complain. When any of them begin to surface, it's time to clean again before you find yourself knee-deep in the clutter of your soul.

Jump In

Those of you who believe in a God of your understanding, and who have faith that the essence of who you are continues on, understand that the life you have here is a brief physical encounter of the eternal soul. Why are you here?

I discovered many years ago that the God of my understanding does not have me on his "need to know" list. The only thing I know is that I am here for a reason, and my job is to jump into life, heart, body, and soul, and do the best I can with whatever circumstances I'm handed.

I no longer believe in happenings by coincidence. A friend once told me that when an individual seeks your help, you've been given an opportunity. If it was supposed to be someone else's opportunity, the individual in need would have called the other person. If someone asks for my help and I tell myself I'm too busy, that I don't want to get involved, and fob them off on someone else, I may be passing up an amazing experience, not only for the other person, but for myself as well.

Throughout my troubled life, others have jumped in, many times literally to save my life. I don't know what others got from the experience, but I will be forever grateful.

Thank God those people were willing to help a stranger. I am standing here, trying to isolate one situation from the many to illustrate my point. How do I distinguish between the man who fed me when I was hungry and the woman who gave me a place to sleep so I wouldn't be on the street and a friend who held my hand through a tragedy?

Every kindness, no matter how seemingly insignificant, is a part of who I am today. There was a time in my life when simply being acknowledged as a human being, being seen, a simple smile and a "Hello," kept me going and made me think there might be some goodness in the world. One of the worst things I can do to another human being is not to acknowledge their existence, to attempt to make him or her feel invisible, not worthy.

When my stepmother died, I traveled to Missouri with my brother to be with our father and to attend the funeral. We stayed at my dad's house, as did other family members. My dad's brother, a favorite uncle of mine when I was growing up, stayed in the same house with me for nearly a week, and never acknowledged my existence. He sat across the dinner table from me and looked through me. He never said one word to me. If he'd slapped me in the face and called me names, it wouldn't have hurt any more than making me feel as if I wasn't worthy of his acknowledgment.

It began when I was released from a mental hospital and started therapy. Because most of my family members were dysfunctional drinkers, the therapist told me he wanted me to take a year and stay away from my family. I didn't just ignore them. I went to each person, tried to explain the circumstances and that I wouldn't be around for a while, and hoped they would understand. Some of them did, others did not. My uncle was one of the ones who did not.

I loved my uncle. I had wonderful memories of him from my childhood, before alcohol consumed his life. He took me fishing, taught me to dive off the high dive at the public pool, and paid attention to me. However, because I could no longer participate in the dysfunction, could not drink with him, I became a nonentity. He died without ever speaking to me again. I hold fast to the love and to the wonderful moments with him that I knew as a child.

Have you ever felt invisible? Do you know what it feels like when someone you care for withholds affection to punish you? Have you done that to another? Look back, think of the circumstances, and remember how you felt or tried to make another feel. Was it worth it?

One thing that kept me from connecting to a God of my understanding for so many years was the knowledge that if I made that connection, I would also have to join the human race. I feared people, letting them into my life and becoming vulnerable to pain or loss. I was an isolated human being even when in a crowd. I think I was the loneliest human being on earth. What I didn't think was that it was my own fault. I told myself that others didn't want me instead of admitting that I didn't think I was good enough to be a part of them, and that as long as I stayed disconnected, I could keep the fear of people hurting me, leaving me, or dying, at bay.

I may have been able to avoid some of the things I feared, but to do so I had to give up all the wonderful experiences and people that might have enhanced my life. I may have jumped in and out of many situations, but I had yet to experience what it means to jump into life.

Spirituality is the safety cord for the big jump. As long as I am connected to that cord, I know I am not alone, that the complete love, forgiveness, and understanding of this God of my understanding will always help me land safely, exactly where I'm supposed to be at that moment. That applies to every circumstance in life, even my death.

Once the connection with a God of your understanding is truly made, you will learn to trust that whatever you do with kindness in your heart can't be wrong. You will listen to your instincts, which I believe is how God speaks to us. You will not hesitate to do what you believe to be the right thing for yourself and for others. You will understand that other people, unless they seek you out, are entitled to choose their own path and make their own decisions. Your connection to God has nothing to do with their connection. It's a personal thing that you cannot do for another, nor can they do it for you.

When you attempt to impose your beliefs on someone, telling yourself you know what's best for them and possibly becoming an enabler of self-destructive behavior, you may be robbing that person of those life experiences needed to learn and progress. If life is a school for the soul, you may be holding back someone you profess to love.

With spirituality comes the ability to let go with love. One of the greatest lessons I've learned over the past few years is that God will let me know when He needs my help, and unless He let's me know, I am to stay in my own business. My business is to make sure the cord is securely attached each day, and jump into life and give it the best I have every moment, in every relationship, whether it be intimate or simply smiling and saying "Hello" to strangers. I am to see what I have, be grateful, and to understand that every moment and every person is important and worthy of whatever I have to offer.

God puts in my path those opportunities that will help me change and grow. It's my job to see them and take action. I always have a choice, but anything I do with meanness in my heart will come back to visit me. I am responsible, not only for my thoughts, feelings, actions, and reactions, but also for making the connection to a God of my understanding.

If you're waiting for a God of your understanding to hook you up to the cord, you may be in for a long wait. The hook is in your hand, and only you can make it work. You must consider honestly where you are in life, how you feel, where you want to be, how you wish to feel, and make a choice. You can continue down the path you have chosen, continue telling yourself you are in control of your life, or hook on and jump in.

TIPS FOR KEEPING IT SIMPLE AND SANE

- Maybe it's time to take a realistic look at the choices that were made in your life and who made them. Even when things beyond your control happen that affect your life, there is a choice of how to react to the situation.

- When you have a spiritual awakening, you open your heart and soul and seek clarity. You live life after a spiritual awakening by understanding that you are never alone and everything that happens is for the best.

- Having faith without making it an active part of your everyday life is like being dropped into the middle of a forest without a map and compass. You may wander around in the hope of finding your way, but still feel frustrated, confused, impatient, and angry.

- It's easy to get excited about uncertainty in life when you have faith, because having faith means that you trust everything will be okay. You will know if you have faith because you will feel it as a part of you. Faith is not ambiguous—either you have it or you don't, and only you know.

→

- A "tell" is the physical manifestation of the truth. It's important to understand tells in yourself and others because they show whether a person is living in truth or conflict.

- Spirituality is the safety cord for the big jump into life, but if you're waiting for a God of your understanding to hook you up to the cord, you may be in for a long wait. The hook is in your hand, and only you can make it work.

Keep It Physically Simple

The most pitiful among men
is he who turns his dreams
into silver and gold.

—Kahlil Gibran

Life after Life?

Many are concerned about whether there is life after death. Books have been written, studies done, and personal experiences shared about the subject. Is there life after death? Who knows. For believers, it's a matter of faith, and for others, it's a matter of proof. For me, the bigger question is, is there life after life?

As I wandered through the cemetery after visiting my oldest son's grave, I thought of the residents there, read their epitaphs, and figured out how old they were according to the dates of birth and death. That's when it hit me. The most important carving on the tombstones was the dash. It really didn't matter when or how they got here, or when or how they died, but what happened in between ... which was indicated by a small dash.

For my son, the dash represented fifteen years of life, and the impact he had on myself and others. I gazed at the tombstones nearby. What did their dashes represent? How did the people they commemorated spend their lives? The epitaphs on the front of the stones were there for the world to see, for appearances, but what of the real people whose bodies lay beneath the soil? Were they really all loving sons, daughters, mothers, fathers, wives, and husbands, or was that just what was put on their tombstones?

Wouldn't it be interesting if the back of the stones were inscribed with the truth of who the people were? My mind wandered to myself, which it often did back in those days. What would the back of my stone say about me? I shuddered. It wasn't pretty. Tears blurred my vision, and I dug in my purse for the bottle I always carried with me. With each drink, I blotted out more of the truth and believed I could walk away and never think of my epitaph again.

The memory of that day haunted my thoughts and dreams and destroyed my living for years. My mind was like a steel trap that had encased all the pain from my past, and no matter how far away I ran, no matter how much drugs and alcohol I used, there was no escape.

Five years after that visit to my son's grave I experienced a moment of clarity. You know the moments I speak of—most of us have them at one time or another. I was 35 years old. I stood in the doorway of a funeral home, reluctant to enter. I didn't like the man who had died, but wanted to support his wife and family. I hated funeral homes; the look and smell of them, the music, and the flowers. It seemed that I had spent the first thirty years of my life burying nearly everyone I cared about, including my children.

The man had died in an alcohol-related car crash, and was a poor father, an abusive, drunken husband, and no friend to anyone. I'd never understood why my friend hadn't left him years before. However, there she stood by the casket, tears streaming down her face, nearly inconsolable. I wondered if she would have "Loving Husband and Father" put on his tombstone and imagined what the back would be like if the truth were told.

As I stepped in and signed the guest book, someone handed me a laminated bookmark with the man's obituary printed on it. I took a seat near the back and read it. Who was this man of whom they spoke? Maybe I was at the wrong funeral. As far as I knew, if he had any good qualities, they were well hidden. I tossed the card on the floor.

The minister started to speak, and from somewhere deep within, something stirred. I felt the pain rise up in me like a tangible object. I fought the tears, but they came. Why was I crying? I wouldn't miss this man. I didn't like him at all. What was wrong with me? That's when I had an epiphany, a simple and striking grasp of reality. That could very well have been me in the casket instead of him.

I picked up the card from the floor and read it again. I looked at those in attendance, his parents, wife, children, friends, and wondered about him. Was he really so different from me? What did I really know about him? I knew he was drunk a lot, and when drunk, he was mean. What I didn't know was what brought him to that point. I'd always excused my rage, my bad behavior, my drinking and drugging, by telling myself I'd had such trauma, so many tragedies, that it was a wonder I had survived, and patted myself on the back for not being worse. I looked down on others like him to make myself feel better. Were we so different? No, except that he was dead and I was still alive. I still had a chance to change the dash between my birth and death, and the time was now.

I must admit, I got really drunk that night. My epiphany was almost more than I could bear. My pain, my anger, and my excuses had lived with me for so long that I wasn't sure I could survive without them. However, this time, I could not drink away my thoughts. I was a mess. My life was a mess. If I died at that moment, who would mourn me? I'd lost or alienated everyone who cared about me. Would anyone really care if I dropped off the face of the earth? What would people say about me? What would my obituary, my epitaph, say if they were honest? I imagined it might be something like:

Obituary

SULLIVAN, ILLINOIS—Barbara Jean (last name optional because she had so many), 35, died draped across an unmade, dirty bed at 1:00 a.m. on Saturday of a drug overdose. If anyone would like to claim the body, contact the county coroner. No services scheduled. Burial will be in a pauper's grave as selected by the county. Barbara was born June 3, 1947, the daughter of Charley and Charline Chaplin. She wandered the United States, did whatever she could for money, and is survived by five ex-husbands. She gave birth to three children, Jon, Nikki, and Ron, and lost one child before birth. She was preceded in death by her mother via suicide, all of her grandparents, many aunts and uncles, all of her children, her pride, her self-esteem, and any self-respect she might have had left. She didn't belong to any organizations or church. If anyone wants to spit on her grave or do a little dance, contact the county for information.

Epitaph

1947–1982
Here lies Barb.
She died the way she lived,
Surrounded by empty bottles.
What she put into life,
Was what she got out of it:
Chaos and misery.

Imagine what your obituary and your epitaph would be if today were your last day. Write it out. When you see something in black and white, it has more impact. If you're not happy with what your dash represents, what would you like to change? Is it possible to change it? Yes—you always have choices, always have the ability to make changes. You simply need to be willing to see the truth, and find those tools that work for you.

The AWE Factor

Have you ever stood in awe of another person's life? I'm not speaking of a person who has great wealth, possessions, or personal appearance, but a person who has overcome great odds in life, and who has come out better for it on the other side. What is it you so admire about that person? Is it their grace and dignity, their compassion for others, their ability to know peace and happiness no matter what is going on outside of them, or perhaps their genuine love of life? Do you wonder what the difference is between you and them? There is a simple secret to their success in life; it's called the "AWE Factor," a concept that is composed of three tools you can use to effect change: awareness, willingness, and effort.

AWARENESS You cannot change what you do not acknowledge as a problem. It's a problem if it affects your life in a negative way. It's a problem if it keeps you from moving forward. It's a problem if it haunts your thoughts and dreams. It's a problem if it causes you problems in any facet of your life. It's not important what others think is your problem, but what you see as a problem.

WILLINGNESS Willingness is about making conscious decisions about any problems that are holding you back from whatever you desire in life. Are you willing to let go of pain from the past, excuses, justifications, and rationalizations, and step out of your comfort zone into the unknown? Are you willing to do whatever it takes to change that dash between life and death?

EFFORT Awareness and willingness mean nothing until you act on them. Once you understand there is a problem, say it out loud, write it down, yell it from the highest mountaintop, or tell it to someone you trust. Do whatever it takes to make it real—get it out of your mind and into the open. When you've done that, and had the willingness to make a decision about how to change your problem, do it. Decisions are funny things. You can make decisions all day long, but until you put them into action, they mean nothing. Remember that any effort you make on your own behalf will only enhance your life in the long run.

Imagine what it would be like if you stood in awe of your own life every day. You can. As long as there is life in your body, there is the opportunity to change that dash between the day you arrive and the day you leave this world. I know this to be true, because I discovered the AWE Factor worked in my own life.

I changed the dash between my birth and death through awareness, willingness, and a lot of effort. It's not easy, but it is simple enough. It only becomes complicated if you are looking for an excuse to avoid taking action. When the reason to make a change becomes bigger than all the reasons not to, you are ready for the AWE Factor.

I came to a realization in considering my potential obituary and epitaph at the age of 35. The realization was that I suffered from the "uns." I was unlovable, unloving, unkind, untrustworthy . . . nearly every "un" you can think of. Because I'd lost so many people in my life, I decided if I didn't love others, if I didn't let them get close to me, I wouldn't have to suffer the pain of loss. I guarded myself by becoming unkind, untrustworthy, and uninvolved. However, there were some unintended consequences for my actions. I may have been safer from the pain of loss, but I also came to know the pain of loneliness, of an empty life. I was miserable, and we all know that misery likes company. I spread my misery around. I resented everyone who had what I didn't, and took it upon myself to try to bring them down to my level.

I looked in the mirror at a face I no longer recognized. The realization was that I'd already died, but since no one knew it yet, they simply hadn't buried me. I hadn't truly lived in years, but had walked through the world like a zombie, and it was do or die time. I said it out loud. I spoke the words over and over until I could no longer deny them. I continued to say them until I felt them. I wept for the person I'd methodically killed little by little.

The decision made, I picked up the telephone, and began calling those people who, underneath it all, I'd stood in awe of, and begged for help. I dropped to my knees and prayed to a God I didn't believe in, and told Him, Her, whatever, all that I'd discovered, and again, begged for help.

One of the most profound things I was told was, "Just because you think something won't work doesn't mean it won't. Look where your best efforts have gotten you." I couldn't argue with that. I became willing to do whatever it took, to listen to others, to open my mind to new ideas, and to seek help wherever I could get it. Anything was better than living the way I had, and imagining dying having lived a totally worthless life.

I dealt with my problems one at a time, one day at a time. It has been twenty-four years since I began this journey inward, which has manifested itself outwardly. I would like to share with you that if I died this day, this moment, what my obituary and epitaph would say, and what my dash would represent.

Obituary

YARNELL, ARIZONA—Barbara Jean Rogers, 59, died from a fall in a climbing accident, 1:00 p.m. on March 1, 2007. She was a costume designer, the founder of Broadway Bazaar Costumes, a published author, and an inspirational speaker. She was a member of the National Costumers Association, the Authors Guild, the Pacific Northwest Writers Association, and can be found in *Who's Who in America.* There will be a wake on Sunday, March 4, at the Cornerstone Bakery, where she loved to eat and socialize, at 9:00 a.m. No flowers please. You may donate funds to women's shelters, animal shelters, or research to fight disease, instead. No burial service. Barbara was born June 3, 1947, the daughter of Charley and Charline Chaplin. She is survived by her husband of twenty-one years, Thomas Rogers Jr., her brother, Bill Chaplin, and her father. She was preceded in death by her children, mother, grandparents, and aunts and uncles. She was a loving, kind wife, daughter, and sister, with friends around the world. She helped wherever she could, whomever she could, whenever she could. She left the world a better place than she found it. She will be missed.

EPITAPH

1947–2007
Here lies Barb
She knew joy,
And passed it on.
She knew love,
And gave it freely.
She lived as she died:
Boldly and unafraid.

I don't know when or how I will die, but I do know how I've lived, so the rest simply doesn't matter. Through the AWE Factor, I changed the dash between life and death, and came to the conclusion that, yes, there is life after life. I no longer have to stand in awe of others because I stand in awe of my life on a daily basis. I have had a life that I couldn't have imagined in my wildest drunken dreams, and I will be forever grateful.

It doesn't matter where you've been in life, what you've done, what you have or don't have; where there is life, there is hope. When you are ready to embrace the AWE Factor, you too can change the dash ... you too can stand in awe of your life.

Beginner's Mind

In the beginning of your life, everything is a new, exciting experience. The sound of a voice and its inflection elicit feelings of security and stimulation, or abandonment and fear. The method of feeding, textures of different foods, and the attitude of the feeder can develop your feelings about the eating experience. How you are touched, if you are held, and how you are handled, whether with kindness and gentleness, or anger and resentment, will determine your bonding experience with others.

In a few short months, you're moving around your world, exploring, touching, pulling yourself up to see what was previously out of your reach. One day, you balance on your tiny feet, and understand what it is to explore from an entirely different place. How others react and deal with your new-found freedom may determine your attitude about independence and consequences.

After a time of being in whatever environment in which you landed, you become accustomed to your surroundings and the people involved. You adapt accordingly. For some, this is a wondrous, fulfilling experience. For others, not so much. Either way, as a child you must learn to survive in your surroundings.

Before you are able to express yourself in words, you feel according to what you see, hear, and touch. Your mind is filled with thoughts, emotions, and often frustrations because of the inability to tell others how to meet your needs.

That's pretty much where my growth, or progression, stopped, and remained for many years. I learned the words, many words, but didn't know how to use them to get my needs met. I tried, but ended up getting my mouth slapped frequently. I stopped trying and learned the fine art of manipulation and contrivance. I learned to play people to my advantage. If that involved lying, cheating, saying whatever I thought they wanted to hear at the time, it was okay as long as my immediate need was met. That is the person I carried into my adult years.

The problem with getting my needs met though cheating, lying, and manipulating is that my satisfaction wasn't real and it didn't last. If I'd lived in a medieval castle, I would have been the court jester. I plastered an expression on my face, acted in a ridiculous manner to get whatever reaction I desired, and moved on to the next person or situation. At the end of the day, costume and makeup removed, all alone, I had no identity. I'd lost myself in the image.

If you could magically transport yourself back in time to a medieval castle, what position would you occupy? Is it the same as the position you held in your family as a child? If not, what is the difference? Did one thing contribute to another? For instance, if you identify with being a servant, under the dominance of a controlling ruler, you might have gone one of two ways, i.e., continued to be subservient, a people pleaser, even a martyr, or changed into a person with control issues, who believes if you are able to control others and your surroundings, you are in control of your life.

Placing yourself in a medieval castle may seem like a strange exercise, but it will tell you a lot about how you see yourself, and may explain why you place importance on certain things. Were you the little prince or princess who was catered to, didn't have to take responsibility or do anything to have your needs met, and believed the expectation of living by rules and boundaries was for others and didn't apply to you? If that was the case, what happened when you emerged into a world that didn't treat you the same? Or, did you fail to launch into the world?

Do you see yourself as a poor cousin, a stable boy, the child of the cook, who watched longingly as others more fortunate indulged themselves? Again, that could affect you in one of two ways, i.e., it could make you determined to work hard to achieve those things you desire, or leave you full of envy and jealousy of anyone who has more than you.

The object of the medieval exercise is to see where you saw yourself in the early years, how it affected you, where you are now, and finally, where you would like to be. How do you get to be where you wish to be? It begins with a beginner's mind. Imagine building your own kingdom, where you are in charge. It will be a novel experience in uncharted territory and new people. You're in charge of the location, and brick by brick, you can build your castle, and surround yourself with others who will enhance your kingdom.

It's called redefining yourself and your life. To redefine is to reexamine and reevaluate with a view to change. Is it really possible? Throughout this book, I've shared bits and pieces of my life with you. However, if you knew everything about me before I changed my life, you would have said, "No way." I say, "Yes, way." The way will require three things: an open mind, brutal honesty, and willingness.

In the three previous sections of this book, I suggested how you might go about changing the way you think, feel, and connect with a power greater than yourself. Those things involve redefining yourself through mental activity. This section is concerned with actually bringing those thoughts, feelings, and faith into your physical world on a daily basis.

To be successful in this endeavor, it will be essential to remember that you are at the beginning of a new path. Like any beginning, it starts with one step forward. It may be a baby step, but it doesn't matter if it is headed in the right direction. Are you saying to yourself that you've left it too late, or that you're too old, or that you're too set in your ways to change? That's simply not true, but if you are looking for excuses not to change, those are certainly handy.

If you decide to look at everything you wish to change, and put an unrealistic expectation on yourself that you can do it all at once, you are setting yourself up for serious disappointment. It took years, and many influences, to become the person you are, to develop the life you live, and it will take time to change. Think of all the things you learned in your lifetime and how long each thing took you to learn it. Tell yourself, "I am a beginner." Each change you make will take as much time as is needed. Start with one thing you want to change.

One of the first things I chose was selfish self-pity. I believed the world revolved around me, and it wasn't doing a very good job. God, the world, and other people had not lived up to my expectations. I didn't see my glass as half full; I saw it as empty. I'd held onto that self-centered misery for as long as I could recall.

I will never forget the woman I sought out with whom I discussed this problem. She'd had a great deal of tragedy and sorrow in her life, but seemed to have overcome her heartache. When I shared my story of woe, trying to elicit a reaction of amazement from her for all I'd endured, she turned to me and said, "What you need is a big dose of gratitude."

When I asked what she meant by that, she repeated, "Gratitude," as if I didn't have enough sense to understand the word, and then, "You need to practice gratitude every day."

I found her attitude and her words offensive. Apparently she hadn't understood all I'd suffered. What in the world did she imagine I had for which to be grateful? I needed to explain. I said, "Yes, but . . ."

"Save your 'yes, buts' for yourself," she said. "You'll need them if you just want to talk about your problem, but are not interested in a solution."

That stopped me in my tracks. Long moments passed as we stared silently at each other. My mind told me to turn, to run, to get away from this person as fast as possible. My misery kept me standing there. I capitulated by asking what the solution of which she spoke was. She replied, "Today, try writing out a gratitude list."

The tears came. What could I possibly write on a gratitude list?

"You have so much," she continued, "but you can't seem to see it because your mind is clouded with self-pity. You need to go home, think about it, and make out the list."

I left, but could not erase the woman's words from my mind. I must have sat down with a piece of paper and a pen in front of me half a dozen times before I finally wrote the first word.

The first word was "recovery." I was sober and drug free, living on my own, and had a support group. It seemed as soon as that one word was written, a light went on. One thing led to another, until I had a list. I've kept that original list over the years, and have returned to it many times. I'd like to share it with you.

I am grateful for: *recovery*
                        food
                        my place
                        job
                        friends
                        clean sheets
                        health

It was a baby step. I didn't have much left in life, but my basic needs were met, which had not always been the case. Somehow, the simple physical effort of putting pen to paper helped me see things in a different way. I called the woman to share my experience. She said, "If you do that each day, you will see the solution."

It's like anything else; if I don't put my thoughts, feelings, and faith into practice, they mean nothing. It has been my habit, from that day to today, to list at least three things each day for which I am grateful.

I discovered that when I live with an attitude of gratitude on a daily basis, it is impossible to feel sorry for myself, and miraculously, I stopped having expectations. With no expectations of what my life should be, there is no disappointment, and I am able to live life on life's terms, take things as they come, and stay in the day.

What are you grateful for today? Try making that all-important list, and when you've completed it, see how you feel. The open-mindedness is trying something whether you believe it will work or not. Brutal honesty is looking past your self-pity to what you actually do have. Willingness is putting pen to paper. This will not change the world around you, but can change your perception of that world.

With each thing you wish to change in your life, there is a solution if you are willing to seek out answers and take that first tentative step. It will be one more brick in the new castle that will be your life. If you build your foundation on talk and air, it will not endure. Action is the mortar that will hold fast your mental, emotional, and spiritual foundation.

The Body

Where you are spiritually will influence your attitude about your body. If you believe the body is all there is, it can become all-important. If you like the appearance of your body, you might become consumed with caring for it to the exclusion of all else. If you are not happy with it, you might work hard to make it better, or see it as the enemy and abuse it.

However, if you see the body as simply the shell you were given to carry the mind, heart, and soul through a lifetime, it will be easier to keep things in perspective. Don't get me wrong, the body is important. Whether you are spiritual or not, it is one of the things that, while making you feel a part of humanity, also enables you to feel unique.

We humans are quite a bunch. We come in all shapes, sizes, and colors, each with our own attributes. I am fascinated with people—their appearance, who they are, what they do, and why. My husband says I've never met a stranger. I guess that's true because I love meeting new people and getting to know them. Because I've chosen to see the body as the carrier of the person, how a person appears on the outside is secondary. I want to know who lives inside the shell.

Have you ever found yourself in a situation with another person who looks so different from you that you become uncomfortable? It is not an unusual occurrence. When I used to take a friend, who happened to be blind, shopping, you would not believe how some people reacted to him. There were those who confused blind with stupid, and even though my friend was looking for a specific item, the clerk would direct his or her questions and answers to me. Others had a tendency to speak loudly and pronounce their words as if, because he couldn't see, he couldn't hear.

When my friend and I were on outings and we encountered the stammering, uncomfortable people, we loved to shock them. Once, in a big discount store, we decided to get a motorized cart because it was difficult for me to lead him and push a basket at the same time. The clerk in charge of the keys looked at us strangely. I said to my friend, "This is the last time I'm letting you drive. Remember the last time. They'll probably never let us back in that store again." The clerk was shocked until we started laughing.

It amazes some people that those with what are considered disabilities actually know about it. It's like if we don't mention he's blind, he doesn't know. I have friends who are little people. They know they are short. I have friends who are disfigured, deformed, some with diseases, others in wheelchairs, and friends of every color. What is it they want from a friend? The same as what you and I want—they want to be loved and accepted just as they are and treated like anyone else. Because, you see, under the skin we are all the same.

I can guarantee you that if you allow yourself to be put off by others because of physical differences, you will miss out on getting to know some really great people. We all have disabilities. Some just show more than others.

Imagine if your disabilities showed on the outside. I had to laugh out loud when I considered what I would have looked like at one point in my life. I pictured myself with a bottle of whiskey fixed to one hand, a cigarette dangling from my mouth, horns protruding from my forehead, crazy looking eyes, and spiked, strangely colored hair. How would you have liked to meet me? I didn't look like that, but it was the reflection I saw in the mirror. I was an addicted, mentally, emotionally, spiritually bankrupt person who did bad things and craved attention. No matter how you look on the outside, what do you see when you look in the mirror? When you are out in the world, are you faking it by trying to look beautiful on the outside when what lives within is totally different? Remember that ugly is as ugly does.

It is wonderful if you have all your parts in good working order and you are attractive to others. There is nothing wrong with wanting to look as good as possible. It only becomes a problem when your insides don't match your outsides. If that's the case, what happens when your body changes? It can happen suddenly through disease, treatment, or a tragic accident. If not, with age, the body simply changes of its own accord. If you believe the body is all-important, a sudden change can be a devastation that lasts a lifetime, not only affecting you, but those around you as well.

When I was going through Graves' disease and the treatment for it, I watched my hair falling out day by day. I had a friend who lived at a distance who was suffering through cancer treatment. When we talked on the phone, our big joke was, "Do you have any hair?" I was down to a thin, stringy mohawk, and she was nearly bald. We laughed together, we cried together, and we developed a bond for which I will always be grateful. She didn't make it, but her spirit, her sense of humor, and her spirituality will live on in me.

She was a beautiful person, inside and out. When her outsides changed, that beautiful person still shined through. She was truly an inspiration to all who knew her. I will never forget one conversation I had with her right before she died. Although very spiritual, she was not affiliated with any religious organization. A preacher one of her well-meaning friends sent to her house knocked on the door. She let him in. In the course of the conversation, he said, "Are you ready?" My friend said, "I've always been ready. Did you think I would leave it until the last minute?" That sums up who she was. She let go of her body with grace, dignity, and peace because she knew it was not all there was to her.

Recently, I watched a show on television about people who are addicted to plastic surgery. They had one procedure after another done, but were never completely satisfied. I had to ask myself if it's the body these people aren't satisfied with, or what lives inside the body. If they are unsatisfied with what's inside of them, then nothing they can do to their outsides is going to make them happy.

One woman in particular caught my attention. She was fighting age with everything she had, as if she could cheat death if she didn't look her real age. Life just doesn't work that way. It doesn't matter how pretty, rich, or important we think we are—none of us will escape the demise of the body. We can fool ourselves, but we can't fool the grim reaper.

Since we have no idea when the body might fail to thrive, or be taken from us suddenly, what is the answer to the body and soul dilemma? I believe my friend had the answer. It is to always be ready. Do not assume there will always be time to change things, to make amends, to get yourself ready. The time to take care of business, to do whatever it takes to match your insides to your outsides, is now.

How do you do that? Think about how much time and effort you spend on your body each day. What if you gave equal time to becoming spiritually fit, or at the least, to making sure that you do not leave things unsaid or undone? I would think that, even if you don't believe in an afterlife, that you have a soul that goes on, if you have one doubt, you might wish to be ready.

It always warms my heart when a catastrophic event takes place and those who have been enemies pull together for the betterment of the whole. They put all their petty differences aside and find perspective. What if we were able to look at each day as a big event? Then, all those little things that seemed so important at the time would lose the power to affect our lives and relationships.

The next time you are faced with a difference between you and someone else, think about it. Ask yourself if you will even remember this difference a year from today. Is the difference important enough to lose a friend or relative over it? What can you do to make the situation better? Be the person who sees each day as a big, important event that could determine your place in an afterlife if one exists. You can either live by the golden rule, i.e., do unto others as you would have them do unto you, or what I call the black rule, i.e., get them before they get you. It's simply a choice.

In my mind, weight is not about size, shape, or density, as much as the weight you may carry inside. I've known skinny people who carried the weight of the world on their thin shoulders. No matter the size of the body, it is the heaviness of the mind, feelings, and spirit that has the greatest impact on quality of life. At the end, if it is the end, when the body falls away, isn't that what's important? Will you leave the world a better place for having been there?

What kind of impact did you have on the lives of others? If a part of you lived on, and had awareness of what was said of you after you died, what would you hear? Wouldn't it be wonderful if you didn't have to die to hear nice things about yourself, to take inventory each day and know you have given your best?

The next time you find yourself in the bathroom fixing your hair, putting on makeup, shaving, or brushing your teeth, take a good look. Look past the reflection of your skin, hair, and features to the person who lives inside. What is the truth of the person who dwells within? When you think of your most beautiful physical attribute, think of your best attribute as a person. Which is more important: big, luscious lips and long eyelashes, or kindness and compassion? The day will come when the lips will deteriorate, but kindness and compassion will never fade away.

No matter the body you live in, the point is to allow the person who lives inside to shine through. If others can't see past your outsides, it's because they are living with their own heaviness and limitations, and the best thing you can do is to leave them to their business and hope someday they will find some understanding. It's not in your power to make others like you. However, what *is* within your power is to put your real self out there, insides and outsides matching, and let the chips fall where they may. Smile from your heart, laugh or cry from your soul, speak your truth, and live every day as a big event.

Relationships

I don't know how many times I've stood at the greeting card section in a store and thought to myself, "Who writes these things?" They have titles like "What is a mother/father/brother/sister/friend, etc.," and then use poetic language to inform the card receiver who and what he or she is supposed to be, and how the card buyer should feel about the relationship. The next question that entered my mind was, what planet did the person being described by these cards come from? He or she didn't live in my world. Thank God they finally came up with humorous, noncommittal cards.

Have you ever had that experience? Did you wonder whom the card writer was talking about? The writer is presenting the ideal of what other people should represent in your life. What happens when others don't live up to the ideal characterization of what they should be to you? Does it make you feel like it might be your fault, that if you had been different, those people important in your life would have liked you more, or treated you better? I hate to be the one to pop your self-important bubble, but it simply wasn't about you.

How could you possibly believe that you could have influenced the people who would raise you? Generation after generation of beliefs, behaviors, and experiences preceded your entrance into the world. You cannot change all that. The best you can hope for is to break the cycle and to change yourself and your perception of others.

When you go out into the world holding fast to the belief that you have the power to change others, you are inviting frustration, disappointment, and unhappiness. Like oil rises to the top in water, who people really are will surface sooner or later, and you will be faced with how little power you have over them. People don't change until they have a reason to change. You might be surprised to know that you can't be that reason. It is an inside job.

You do not have a choice of family members, but you do have the choice to interact or not interact with each individual. If you choose to include a family member in your life, and you want to have a good relationship, the key is total acceptance without compromising yourself. It takes two to play the game. If your relative is trying to manipulate you through guilt or shame, or lays expectations on you that you are not comfortable with, you can simply refuse to participate. If you help another, in any way, it should be because you want to do it, not because you feel you have been forced into it. When you compromise, you will end up not only resenting the other involved, but also yourself.

On the other hand, don't expect others to compromise for you. I'm a firm believer that you can't have it both ways. Whatever you expect from others, you should be willing to give them. The only way to know these things about each other is through clear communication. Others cannot read your mind. I know it's more difficult to say the words with a family member, but it is important to maintain a healthy relationship.

The wonderful thing about friends is that you have a whole world of people from which to pick. It is human nature to be attracted to, or attractive to, those people who are in a similar place, mentally, emotionally, spiritually, and physically, as you. That's not a problem unless you are in a bad place. For instance, the last thing I desired in a friend when I was acting out in the party scene was some buzz kill who gave me disapproving looks and made comments I didn't want to hear. God forbid I would have a healthy friend at that time in my life. I couldn't handle it . . . you know, the truth.

Reflect on your life. As you entered different phases in your life, who were your friends? Did your group of friends change as you changed? As I think back, there are very few people who have traveled with me through the years, through all my strange phases. I can count them on one hand. They were the friends who truly cared for me, who loved me many times in spite of myself, and who I always knew would tell me the truth. The sad thing was that I would go through periods of staying away from them because I didn't want to hear the truth and took them for granted. My true friends were those who loved me until I was able to love myself.

Today, I understand that there are all kinds of friendships, and that I can keep them separated and clear in my mind. There are those people I have something in common with, i.e., writing, costuming, addiction, even health problems. Our conversations tend to revolve around a mutual interest. There are those whom I wave to, sit down with at a restaurant if we both happen to be there, and share my life with on a superficial basis. My close friends are those who have taken the time to know me inside and out, as I have them, and we like each other anyway. They are the ones with whom I can think out loud and never feel the need to censor my thoughts or feelings. There are not many, but they are of great value in my life.

Who are your friends? What type of friend is each one? Do you enhance that person's life? Is your life enhanced because that person is a part of it? When you see your friend or hear from him or her, does it warm your heart, or do you cringe when you see that person walking up to your door or on caller ID? It's important to look at this realistically because it's a part of keeping your life simple, uncluttered by relationships that no longer serve a positive purpose in your life.

Situations and people change, and you will go through many changes. People grow, many times in different directions. Therefore, there will be times when you will have to make a conscious decision to end a friendship, or allow another to walk away from you. How will you go about it? Because I hated honest confrontation, I came up with all kinds of inventive ways to get rid of that person I no longer wanted in my life. I could have written a book on all the unhealthy ways I ended friendships. Have you found some creative ways that didn't involve telling the truth? Although you might feel relief that the person is out of your life, how do you feel about yourself? Do you feel like a liar, a coward, a fraud? Then, there is the ugly process of having to figure out justifications and rationalizations to excuse your behavior. Way to complicate your life.

Do you keep from speaking the truth to a friend for fear of their reaction? Do you tell yourself you don't want to hurt that person? It took some of those painful truths, told to me by courageous, real friends, to encourage me to go on that brutally honest inside journey. Which do you think is kinder: my friend shaking her head and telling others, "Barb's a mess. I wonder what it will take for her to wake up? I hate to see what's going to happen to her," or her telling me, "You're a mess. What's it going to take? When are you going to wake up? I don't want to be a part of your self-destruction. I don't want to live in your drama."

I had that very thing happen one day with the woman I considered my best friend. At that moment, I hated her, called her vile names, and threw her out. I thought of everything bad about her that I could and told myself she had no right to judge me. I felt betrayed and alone, but mostly, although I wouldn't admit it, scared. The fear showed itself as anger, but the truth was, deep down I knew she was right. It was the grandest favor she ever did for me. It took time, but as I changed, I had the opportunity to regain her love and trust, and we are still friends all these years later. I will be forever grateful to her. Real friends don't talk *about* each other—they talk *to* each other.

What are those things friends have told you that touched a nerve, that you reacted to badly, but later understood how much love and courage it took for them to put their fears aside and show you the kindness of truth? Have you ever gone back to them and told them how grateful you are? Did you learn the life lesson from them of how to be a real friend? Do you talk about friends, or talk to friends? These are the questions you need to ask yourself to determine what you actually are as a friend.

Loving and Living Separately

As important as family and friends are, the relationship that seems to be uppermost on most people's minds is a romantic one, i.e., falling in love, being loved, by a stranger. I had a friend who once told me that I was a love addict. I was either falling in love, devastated by love, falling out of love, or looking for new love. I got high on the drama of love. Other than grief, I can't think of another emotion stronger than love. Come to think of it, grief is a form of love. You might be thinking that hate can be stronger than love. But isn't hate nothing more than love despoiled?

Don't confuse passion with love. Passion can be a part of love, but it is not the be-all and end-all of love. You can be physically attracted to many others, absolutely passionate with some, but those of you who have experienced true love will know the difference. The difference is that when the physical body grows older, when passion wanes, true love endures. It becomes that warm, comfortable feeling of coming home when you are with the one you love. It's when the touch of a hand from that one special person is better than all the passion in the world.

Because of the way I grew up, my personal experiences, and all the loss in my life, I did not believe there was such a thing as lasting love. Maybe I wasn't a love addict as much as simply a drama queen, and relationships afforded me the opportunity to indulge my love of drama. I was 20 years old when love struck me. I say it that way because it happened suddenly, and it scared the hell out of me. When I met this man, who, by the way, was not my type at all, I had already been married twice, was working on a third, and had given birth to three children. What I'm trying to say is that I was no virgin. To say I had intimacy issues is an understatement. I never let myself get too close to anyone for fear of the pain I would feel when it ended, and I knew it would end . . . it always ended.

Every time I saw this man, our eyes met, and he spoke to me, an unfamiliar, uncomfortable feeling began in the pit of my stomach and traveled throughout my body. I told myself I simply wasn't thinking straight. All I had to do was get away from him and the feeling would pass. I ran. I moved out of state. I married other men. I got divorced. I moved some more. However, no matter where I went, whom I was with, or what I was doing, this man lived in my mind and my heart. He was the first thing I thought of in the morning and the last thing I thought of at night.

By the time I got my fifth divorce and was in recovery from my addictions, the fear of being with anyone was so huge I figured I would spend the rest of my life alone. The problem was that I'd never resolved my feelings for this man. Part of my recovery program was to make amends to those people I'd harmed. I'd done some pretty nasty things to this man and decided I would find closure when I faced him, made my amends, and resolved my feelings.

As life has a way of doing, it didn't quite work out that way. As soon as he walked into the coffee shop, nearly seventeen years after I'd met him, the same feelings overwhelmed me. I had never felt that way before, or since. What was I to do?

I sought counsel from a dear friend, who was dying at the time. She told me that when I quit taking risks in life, I had also quit living. She pulled the covers back on her bed and said, "You might as well climb in here with me." Her opinion, which I trusted, got me thinking. The truth was that I was in love with this man, I would always be in love with him, and I had a choice. The choice was to live alone, in fear, protecting myself, or to use my new-found faith in a God of my understanding, myself, and my love. I chose to walk through the fear, and have been married to the love of my life for over twenty-one years.

Falling in love is easy. Living happily with another human being on a daily basis is an art. There were a lot of false starts, mistakes, and pain in my life before I discovered the secret. The secret that eluded me for so long is to live separately together. It works in every type of relationship.

Once you are of an age of choice, living on your own, you can implement the art of living separately together in your life. Even if you are older and have lived a lot of life, but are not satisfied with your relationships, you might want to give it a try.

The concept is simple. It means to be exactly who you are no matter whom you are with, where you are, and what you're doing. It means that you have a right to your passions and dreams as much as anyone else. In grown-up relationships, one person should not have power over the other. Adults do not feel the need to make excuses and explain what it is they wish to do or not do. Mutual respect and common decency are a part of all communications.

In each relationship there are two points of view, and each person involved should feel free to express their point of view without fear of reprisal. If you've ever been in a relationship in which you always feel like you are walking on eggshells, you will understand how important it is to be able to openly and honestly express yourself. If you've ever been in a relationship in which you felt the need to be someone you are not, to change who you are to suit another, you have known repressed anger and frustration.

How do you combat these pitfalls? Begin the way you wish to continue. Too many times when people meet, they act in ways they believe will make them more attractive to the other person. Remember the oil to water scenario? It applies to everyone. It's unfair to act one way when you're dating and then to change after a commitment is made. Be who you are from the beginning, and avoid confusion and unrealistic expectations. If the other person likes you, or perhaps falls in love with you, it will be the real you, not some façade you are hiding behind.

Once you're in a committed relationship, either married or living together, hang on to yourself. Stay in your business, and allow the other person his or her business. Treat the other person involved as an adult who has the mental capacity to make choices, and insist that you are afforded the same respect. You do not have to like the same things, share friends, hobbies, or even religion and politics. Being individuals who share space but have separate interests can keep life interesting. The happier you are as an individual, the more stimulated you are, the deeper the relationship.

When you are able to give up the need to control another, mold yourself into something you're not, and accept another's right to be who they are, you will know what it means to live separately together. The next opportunity you have to begin a new relationship, whether it's a friendship or more, give it a try. I think you will be pleasantly surprised, as will the other person. If it doesn't work out, you will know that you went into it with integrity, and you can exit the same way.

You can be a part of your world, the community in which you live, your family, your friends, and committed relationships, and practice living separately together. When you are able to successfully practice this concept, you will know what it is to be uncluttered by lack of focus and confusion. You will know who you are and present the truth to the world.

Communications

Availability, or lack of availability, changes the value of things. A collector knows that items made in limited editions, which are more difficult to find, are more desirable, and therefore more valuable. For those who have plenty, a bowl of rice is simply a side dish to be eaten, left, or tossed out, depending on their taste and desire. For those without much, that same bowl of rice can be the difference between life and death, and thus takes on great value.

We live in a world of electronic communication, which is supposed to make our world smaller and bring us together. Televisions, computers, cell phones, Blackberries, etc., have become common items. They allow us instant communications, facts about anything at our fingertips, ways to buy and sell, and entertainment at the press of a button. All those things can be wonderful and enhance our lives. However, like everything else in life, there can be a downside.

Recently, as I've worked with others who are having problems with relationships, whether it's at work, with friends, with family, or with love, I've discovered the downside of electronic communication. In some cases, instead of bringing people together, it has enabled them to become more isolated, not only from the world and other people, but also from their own selves. Now that children are growing up with electronic communication, the trend has become more extreme.

Many of the young adults, 25 years old and under, whom I deal with regularly, have developed a codependency problem with machines and expect immediate gratification. I find myself saying things like, "Dumping someone in a text message is not acceptable," or "Have you actually talked to the other person involved . . . you know, face-to-face?" It's like, if they do these things electronically, they remove themselves from the emotions involved. In a way, they do. It's easier to punch a few buttons than to look into the face of pain, confusion, or devastation.

I know of one young couple that lives in the same house, but when either is angry with the other, they email each other. They live in the same house! I imagine it is easier to email, to remove yourself from the situation, and to say those things you are apparently incapable of saying as you gaze into another person's face and are confronted with their emotions, but what is the end result? If it was you on the other end, would you find resolve, or see that person using technology to communicate with you as cowardly, and lose respect for him or her? If you are guilty of the great electronic cop-out, how do you feel about yourself?

Easier isn't always better. Do you cope with life, its problems and relationships, electronically? Do you use TVs, computers, and electronic games to avoid your thoughts? Have they become your companions, taking the place of interaction with real people and allowing you to avoid feelings of emptiness and loneliness? Do you say things in text messages or emails that you would be uncomfortable saying in person? These are questions to consider if you have a problem with the art of healthy communication.

Communicating is a skill. A skill is honed through practice; to practice is to be actively engaged. Are you actively engaged with yourself; your thoughts, feelings, and beliefs? In other words, do you know who you are? That may seem like a strange question, but you might be surprised at how many struggle with this problem. To avoid communicating with yourself and getting to know who you are is to put yourself at risk for confusion, frustration, and unhappiness, all of which can lead to self-destructive behavior. It's impossible to like yourself if you don't know and accept yourself.

How do you communicate with yourself? The first thing to do is to eliminate noise and outside stimulation. Some call it "quiet time," others say "meditation," and I call it "time alone with my thoughts." Did you immediately think that you don't have the time for meditating and the like? You make time for what is important, and this is definitely important. There are many times throughout the day when you can take a few moments to be alone with your thoughts. Try turning off the radio, tape player, CD player, and cell phone while driving. It's just you, your thoughts, and absolute quiet—a good time to think. The bathroom can be a wonderful place of solitude. Leave the paper, magazines, and other forms of distraction outside the door. Turn your iPod off while you walk or do other exercise. Avoid electronics on days off and during vacation time. You don't have to set a particular time, roll out a mat, sit in an awkward position, and chant to be alone with your thoughts. You can do it whenever and wherever you choose.

The more comfortable you are with yourself, the more adept you will be at communicating with others. After all, it's difficult to share yourself with another if you don't know whom you are sharing. That thought brings back a lot of bad memories from my past. I didn't have a clue who I was for years, and frankly, was afraid to find out. I would do almost anything not to be alone with my thoughts and feelings. If the kind of electronics that are available today had been available at that time in my life, I would have totally abused them, and used them any way I could to avoid being alone with myself.

One of the most difficult times in my life was when I first got into recovery from addiction. I didn't end up in a nicely furnished treatment center, surrounded by people in the same boat and understanding counselors. I had no supportive family members left, most of which was my own fault. I'd buried all my children. There were no husbands, boyfriends, or friends willing to stand by me. For the first time in my life, I was totally alone, except for those people whom I met in meetings.

I lived in a remodeled half of a garage, with the other half still a garage. Since I'd lost everything, there was no television, radio, air conditioning, or even a telephone for quite some time. I was not only totally alone, but in total quiet as well. I hated that—over the years I had done almost anything not to be alone, not to face the silence. I spent time with people I didn't like, doing things I didn't want to do, in places I wouldn't have been caught dead in sober, and passed out at night.

I thought it was the worst of times, but today I know that because of those early years, I was forced to look at myself, to get to know myself. Deprivation can be a great teacher. For nearly a year, I suffered from insomnia. The nights were long and the quiet was deafening, except for my mind, which seemed to be working overtime. Clarity came slowly, but it did come, many times in the wee hours of the morning while the rest of the world slept. Although my quiet time was imposed on me through circumstance, that takes nothing away from the benefits I received. I will forever be grateful for those few years of struggle that forced me to learn to communicate with myself.

What would your life be like if you turned off those things you use for distraction and avoidance? Imagine not being able to so much as pick up a telephone to make a call, or push a button for entertainment? What kind of effect would that have on you and your way of life? Try it for an hour, a few hours, or for the very adventurous, a day. You might be surprised at the result.

Communication with others lies in the ability to transmit information, thoughts, or feelings, so that the communication is understood. If you don't understand those things about yourself, how can you possibly communicate them effectively to another? In a face-to-face communication, there is more involved than words. Feelings are expressed in the eyes, body language, and demeanor. How do you transmit those things on a machine?

The point of this chapter is to help you think about how you communicate, and what methods you've chosen to use. There is so much available to you today that the choices seem unlimited. The key word is "choice." Simply because something is available doesn't mean you have to use it. The value of electronic communication is the ability to see the true value, keep it in perspective, and not fall into machine abuse until it controls your life. When, and if, you decide to take some time alone with your thoughts, you might consider these questions:

- Am I confused or comfortable with who I am?

- Am I able to honestly share myself with others or do I hide behind electronics?

- Am I fearful of face-to-face confrontation?

- What am I willing to do to avoid being alone?
- Do I use electronics for noise to avoid quiet time?
- How much of my communication with others revolves around machines?
- How would I react if electronic communication devices were removed from my life?
- Am I addicted to electronic communication?

These questions are but a few that you might think about if you are unhappy with your communication skills, if, with all that is available to you, you continue to feel isolated from others and the world. Only you know how you feel, and can answer these questions for yourself.

For me, there is nothing better than face-to-face communication. I want to look into your eyes, see your happiness, share your pain, and understand who you are through honest sharing. I want you to know me, the real person standing before you just as I am. Someone once told me, "You can hide from others, you can hide from the world, but you can't hide from yourself forever. The truth will come out, if not in words, in your actions." What do your actions tell you about yourself?

Finances

Part of eliminating the clutter that may be overwhelming your life involves your finances. The symptoms of financial clutter are a constant feeling of pressure and stress. The solution is clarity and living within your means.

You do not have to be a math wizard to figure out where you stand financially. It's a matter of basic math. You have a certain amount of money coming in, another amount going out, and the difference between the two. Why, then, can it be so difficult for some to manage that simple idea?

Believe me when I tell you that I understand financial problems. As a single teenaged mother with very little education, I found myself in situations in which I had to do some desperate, disgusting, even illegal acts to care for myself and my son. I suffered from constant pressure and stress to survive. It affected not only me, but also my child.

However, it's not only the poor who suffer from financial clutter. It seems to be a great problem with the working middle class, and in some cases, the wealthy. Some would say it is the easy availability of credit that is the problem. I would say it is the choice to use credit that is the problem. It's easy to understand the need to feed yourself or your children, but much more difficult to have compassion for those who suffer from the wants without the means.

For those who suffer from the wants without the means, it's not really about the material things. It goes much deeper than that. Many years ago, I cleaned house for a single woman who was around 60 years old. Throughout her house, I discovered stashes of brand-new items, still in their original boxes, that she had never used. As time went on, the stashes grew as she went further into debt. She eventually had to let me go because she could no longer afford to have someone else clean her house. Later, I heard she had filed for bankruptcy, and died in the same house surrounded by stacks of unopened boxes and piles of catalogues.

I didn't get it. I judged her harshly, appalled at the idea of buying useless items instead of paying bills. It wasn't until I began working with addiction that I realized her addiction for shopping was as serious as my addictions. Shopping, the excitement of receiving parcels in the mail, was her fix. Talking to people on the phone, even just to order an item, kept her from feeling lonely. I used chemicals to assuage my loneliness; she used shopping. Is it really that different?

For others, the wants without the means is about comparison, envy, and image. It's more commonly known as "keeping up with the Joneses." I didn't suffer from that personally, mainly because I had no credit for so many years, but I suffered from it emotionally. I bankrupted myself trying to fit in with a world that I didn't believe would ever accept me.

I looked around at those with "normal" lives, wanted what they had, did some bizarre things to get what I most desired, but it didn't work because it wasn't real.

Realistically speaking, to purchase anything, especially something you don't want or can't afford, to make you feel better about yourself will not work. Oh, it will at first. There will be that moment of exhilaration in the beginning, but sooner or later, it will be replaced by pressure and stress. And what will you do when someone else acquires an item you can't afford? There will always be someone with more.

Another reason a person might get into financial clutter is the belief that others will bail them out. Do you think I'm talking about some rich kid whose parents pay through the nose to keep him or her out of financial trouble? That may be true in some cases, but what of those who give no thought to who is paying through the nose for their lack of responsibility?

I never considered who paid for my shoplifting, my car wrecks with no insurance, those urgent stops in emergency rooms because my body could no longer handle what I was putting into it, or my stay in the mental hospital. After my release from the mental hospital, the State paid for my education and living expenses. When I say the "State," I mean you and your taxes. Somehow I got it into my head that because I'd had a tough life, you owed me something. It became a game to see how much I could get for nothing.

When I got into recovery from my addictions, I had to learn what it meant to be financially responsible. The first thing I discovered was that nobody "owed" me anything. It was time to give up my addiction to drama, to living on the edge, to feeling as if I was alive because I could con someone into taking care of me. I think the comment that made me stop and take inventory of who I'd been and what I'd done was, "What makes you think you are any better than the rest of us? We work, we pay our taxes and bills, and we accept that it is a part of real life."

I'd always excused my behavior by telling myself I didn't feel like I was accepted by others, by the world—that I didn't fit in with you. I didn't, but whose fault was it? I wanted what you had, but was not willing to do what you did. I said I wanted to be "normal," but those who live normal lives work, pay their bills, pay taxes, buy insurance, and accept what has to be done.

Another revelation I had through not so gentle suggestions was that for everything I took from life, I cheated another out of an opportunity. There may have been a person with legitimate problems who desperately needed what I received. Today, when others ask me why I spend so much time working with others in crisis and in addiction, I tell them it's because I can never give back all I've taken. I raped the world, and I want to make amends.

What about you? Do you suffer from the pressure to earn more, to find a way to pay for those things you think you must have? Do you live in constant stress over money issues? Are you a financial clutter junkie? If you think that may be the case, try this twelve-question, yes-or-no quiz, and find out.

1. Are you in over your head financially, but keep adding more debt?
   ❏ YES   ❏ NO

2. Do you find yourself borrowing, with no idea how to pay the money back, then having to lie and avoid those you owe?
   ❏ YES   ❏ NO

3. Have you tried how-to books, tapes, etc., to get yourself out of financial problems, only to fall back on old habits?
   ❏ YES   ❏ NO

4. Do you do whatever it takes to hide your financial problems?
   ❏ YES   ❏ NO

5. Do you indulge in other addictions to escape stress caused by financial problems?
   ❏ YES   ❏ NO

6. Do you get a high from shopping, but it doesn't last?
   ❏ YES   ❏ NO

7. When you get a bill, do you tell yourself if you can't pay it all, you won't pay any of it, and spend the funds inappropriately?
   ❏ YES   ❏ NO

8. Do you take your financial problems to bed, and awaken with them in the morning, feeling unrested?
   ❏ YES   ❏ NO

9. Do you compare yourself with others, and believe there is something wrong with you?
   ❏ YES   ❏ NO

10. Is stress and pressure from your debts affecting your relationships?
    ❏ YES   ❏ NO

11. Are you unhappy with the way you live?
    ❏ YES   ❏ NO

12. Are you a financial clutter junkie who believes you are in so deep that there is no way out?
    ❏ YES   ❏ NO

If you answered yes to up to three of the questions, you are well on your way to a serious problem. If you answered yes to any more than three, you have arrived. The good news is that when you are ready to admit the problem and do something about it, there is a simple solution.

It may be a simple solution, but that doesn't mean it's an easy solution. It will require a drastic change in your lifestyle. How do you get started? You've begun when you acknowledge your problem. The next step is to stop. For one day, stop doing those things that feed into your problem. For instance, if you order items through the Internet or TV, turn them off. Are catalogues a problem? Get rid of them—all of them. If you go to the post office and receive new ones, don't bring them into your house. Stay away from dangerous people and places. If you have friends with similar financial problems and attitudes, stay away. If you can't go into the mall without buying anything, don't go. Just try it for one day.

Since you have more time to do other things, it might be a good time to sit down with all your paperwork and figure out where you are financially. Write it out in black and white, and take a good look at it. Don't plague yourself with questions about how you can handle it all at once or what you will do tomorrow or next week, next month, or next year. That will only defeat the purpose. The purpose of writing it out is that you can't know where you want to go until you understand where you are. However, do not forget to stay in the day.

Each day is a new beginning, and you can only accomplish in that day what you are able. If, in the beginning, the best you can do is not add to the problem, it's a start. It's like you've dug yourself into a hole; if you keep digging, you will never get out. It may take some time and effort to extricate yourself, but at least you aren't going farther in. You may think you're tough, that you can do it on your own, but apparently what you've been doing hasn't worked so far, so why would you think it would this time? It has been my experience that most people need help. Many do not seek help because it's one thing to admit the problem to themselves, but a whole other thing to say it out loud to others. Do not let false pride and fear of embarrassment keep you from seeking whatever help you require to find a better way of life.

Help is not borrowing more money from friends, or trying to fix everything at once with a quick loan. You didn't get into your situation in a day, and you will not get out of it quickly, either. For most, it will be a slow, step-by-step experience. I've come to believe, through my own experiences with addiction, that it's important to go through the process, as difficult as it may be, as a reminder never to return to the addiction.

Although there are many roads to recovery from any, and all, addiction, I chose a 12-step program that has worked well for me for nearly twenty-five years. Just as there are anonymous meetings for alcoholics and drug addicts, gamblers, those with eating disorders, sex addicts, smokers, clutterers, there are meetings for those addicted to debt. (See the end of this chapter for more information.) In these meetings, there is no need to feel out of place, embarrassed, or humiliated because everyone else there has the same problem or they wouldn't be there. In meeting others with the same problem, you will discover you are not crazy, and you are not alone in your struggle.

There is no magic plan that will instantly turn you around, but there are twelve suggested steps, and suggestions from others who have already been down the road you have chosen to travel, to direct you to the solution. All that is required of you is an open mind and the willingness to try things, even when you don't think they will work. After all, your best efforts have put you in your present position. What have you got to lose?

You will hear about a Higher Power, or a God of your understanding, in 12-step meetings. Again, it's about trying things even if you are not convinced. Can you pray for money? I was always a little leery of praying for money. The way my luck had run, I figured God would drop it on my head in pennies. I decided it was better to try praying for a way to earn money and the willingness to see it. Granted, this Higher Power had some strange ideas about what I should be doing, but it never failed to work, and to be for my best interests in the long run. I wasn't far in debt, but I had no money or assets, and no credit. It took me nearly five years, step by step, to turn my life around.

Addiction is like living with a monster inside that can only thrive in the darkness. Once brought out into the light of day, the monster loses power. Money and possessions have no power, except the power you give them. It's simply a matter of deciding what you want in life, what you are willing to give up for it, and doing whatever it takes to live in the solution. If it takes going to meetings, counseling, therapy, or whatever your choice is, get help. If it takes carrying a notebook with you every day and keeping track of what you spend and where, do it. If you can't think of anything else to pray for, pray for the willingness to do whatever is needed. The solution is in taking action.

Life is only as difficult as we make it. There will be enough to deal with that life itself throws at us. Why make it worse by giving away our happiness and peace to temporary items, paper, and the illusion of power?

I refuse to believe this life is about nothing more than work and worry, pain, and suffering. I have one rule of thumb: when I begin to feel overwhelmed, I stop, take a reality check, and eliminate those things that are affecting my life negatively. I get into action, doing whatever I can to bring myself back to a livable, happier place.

If you have a debt problem, and are sick and tired of being sick and tired, you might give Debtors Anonymous, or DA, a try. They can be contacted at:

Debtors Anonymous
General Service Office
P.O. Box 920888
Needham, MA 02492-0009
(781) 453-2743
www.debtorsanonymous.org

Living Space

Where you live is influenced by family ties, availability of work, finances, and health. When any of those things change, it can cause a transition. How you live is determined by where you are mentally, emotionally, physically, and spiritually. As any, or all, of those things change, how you live will be altered.

Part of my fascination with people includes where they live, how they live, and why. The intrigue began when I was young, poor, and moving from one horrible place to another, living hand to mouth. I used to walk down a street, or drive into a neighborhood when I had a car, and look at the houses filled with families and things, and it became my idea of what it meant to live a normal life. I felt like a child with no money, gazing longingly into the window of a candy store. My mouth watered for it as if I could imagine the taste of it. My belly growled with hunger for it. My hand pressed against the glass that allowed me to see, but not obtain, it. With every fiber of my being, I wanted to know that feeling of coming home to a real home and a normal life.

Have you experienced that feeling of always being on the outside, looking in? Do you know what it is to be a part of something, but not to feel as if you belong? Do you tell yourself that if you had been brought up in a different family, had more money, had a better job, or were more physically able, you wouldn't feel those things? That's what I told myself for years, but the truth was that I used those things as excuses not to change. I was the glass that separated me from what I said I most desired, but I was not willing to do those things required for a better way of life.

What is required? A clean sweep; uncluttering your mental, emotional, physical, and spiritual issues. For me, the first step was physical. Before I could consider anything else, I first had to remove from my body all the mind-altering substances and regain my health and the ability to think rationally, as much as was possible. I may not have been able to undo some of the damage I'd already done, but I could avoid doing any further damage.

What are you putting into your body or using to alter your mind? How do you cope with stressful situations or simply the demands of everyday life? Do you drink to escape? Do you take pills to relieve stress or to sleep? Do you overindulge in foods for comfort? Are you starving yourself to have some semblance of control in your life? There are other things I haven't mentioned, but no matter, because what you're doing is not as important as why you're doing it and how it is affecting your body, your mind, and your way of life.

I bet you were thinking this chapter would be about how to clean and organize your living space. It may surprise you to know that is exactly what it's about. Your living space is where you are at any given time. The one constant, no matter where you live, is you. Until you unclutter yourself, it really makes no difference if you live in one room or a mansion, or whether you're clean or messy. Take it from someone who, although having lived in many different types of housing, finally understands what it means to come home.

"Home" is that place where you can leave the distractions of the world outside the door, feel safe and secure, loved and nurtured, think, feel, and act with no pretense, and rest your body, mind, and soul. I will never forget the first time I had that feeling. I walked into a 12-step meeting, and someone there said, "Welcome home." I was taken aback, but soon discovered it was the beginning of my journey home.

A group of strangers made me feel at home until I was able to bring myself to that point. They shared their stories, many of which were different from mine. The similarities were in the feelings. They'd lived behind the glass, just as I had, and they'd found a way in. Between their suggestions and the 12 steps, I finally had some answers, but applying them was another thing. I was assailed by fear, doubt, and more questions. One thing I found out was that when I didn't like the answers, I conjured up more questions.

Do you do that? Do you move from one person to the next, latch on to different ideas until they involve willingness and effort to change, and move on quickly, seeking an easier, softer way? When the answer seems simple, do you complicate it by picking it apart and questioning every-thing? Do you tell yourself that something so simple can't work for you because you're different, and your life is too complex? Are you comfortable in your cluttered living space behind the glass?

I'd gotten a glimpse of what it was like on the other side of the glass when I physically cleared my space, and I wanted more. The mere thought of a mental and emotional clean sweep nearly put me back on the other side. Being an extremist who lived for immediate gratification, I wanted to jump over to the other side of the glass and have everything happen at once. It doesn't work that way. It's like learning a new language, a musical instrument, or any other unfa-miliar skill. The tools I would need are teachers who have honed their skills, instructions, and the willingness to prac-tice every day. If I read a pamphlet and convinced myself I knew it all, argued with and questioned those who did, and refused to practice, following the step-by-step instructions, do you honestly think I would learn anything? To achieve my goal of a clean sweep, it would require putting all my preconceived ideas, ways of thinking, and feelings aside, and becoming teachable.

If you read the first three sections of this book, you know what I became willing to do to clean my living space. How badly do you want to clean your space? What are you will-ing to do? As they say in 12-step programs, "If you want what I have, do what I did." What do I have? I have a life uncluttered by the past, free of fear, anger, and resentment; I know peace, and I am home wherever I happen to be at the moment.

The steps I, and many others, used to deal with addictions can be used for any problem life throws at me. After all, only the first step mentions alcohol. It can be tweaked to suit your specific problem. For instance, "I admit I am powerless over (fill in the blank), that my life has become unmanageable." The following steps are a set of suggested instructions that have never failed to help me find a solution. The remaining steps, made personal, might look something like this:

STEP 2: Came to believe a power greater than myself could restore me to sanity.

STEP 3: Made a decision to turn my will, and my problem, over to a God of my understanding.

STEP 4: Made a searching and fearless moral inventory of myself.

STEP 5: Admitted to God, to myself, and to another person the exact nature of my part in the problem.

STEP 6: Asked God to remove the defect in my character that added to the problem.

STEP 7: Asked God to remove that shortcoming so that it never becomes a problem again.

STEP 8: Made a list of any harm I caused, and became willing to make amends.

STEP 9: Made those amends without causing further harm.

STEP 10: Continued to examine my actions, and when wrong, promptly admit it.

STEP 11: Stayed in daily contact with a God of my understanding, asking for guidance, and the willingness to listen and act.

STEP 12: Having had a spiritual awakening as the result of living my life in solutions instead of problems through these steps, to share these principles when I am called upon.

If you doubt what I'm saying, try taking one problem through these steps, and see the results. As you resolve each problem in your life and put it behind you, you will know what it means to unclutter your living space so that you will feel at home no matter where you are.

Now it's time to speak of your surroundings. Let's take a walk through your current place of residence. How do you feel about allowing me, or anyone else, to take a good look around?

Are you comfortable, or do you spend the walk-through making excuses because things aren't the way you want them to be? How do you think they should be? Why aren't they? Try touching each item in a room, and telling me exactly what it means to you, or how you use it. Does it mean anything to you? Do you use it? When was the last time you used it? Honestly answering these questions is the beginning of dealing with clutter.

Clutter is useless items that impede movement and reduce effectiveness. Just as mental, emotional, and spiritual clutter keeps you from moving forward and allowing new, exciting ideas and ways of living into your life, so does physical clutter. Opening your space and clearing away the old and useless, allows room for the new, the different, and will help you get excited about not only your residence, but your time there as well.

I am not a domestic goddess who enjoys cleaning, cooking, or entertaining at my house. It is my sanctuary, where I can write, reflect, spend time with my husband and pets, and, if I choose to do so, run around naked. It's an old house that wanders up the side of a mountain. We've spent ten years developing this old house into our home. The changes included ripping out all the old carpeting and replacing it with tile and wood floors, which I can sweep with a broom. I tiled the kitchen surfaces, even the inside of the sink, to avoid constant cleaning. The shower is a circular horse trough with a shower curtain that hangs from the ceilings. It requires little cleaning. We use recyclable paper plates because I hate to do dishes. That's right, I don't own a dish. For cooking, I have two saucepans, two skillets, and a soup pot. That's all we need. You get the idea. Although I like a clean, clutter-free house, I have other things that I want to do, so I set the household up to accommodate me instead of me accommodating it.

Tell me about your house. Try writing it out as if you were going to submit it to one of those home and garden magazines. But you have to tell the truth. After you've written down a description, read it. Have you fixed up your house to accommodate you or are you a slave to things you don't really wish to have or do? What changes can you make to take your power back from a house that you are allowing to abuse you? My answer is to decide what things will fulfill your basic needs, get rid of anything that has no real meaning to you, and cater to what works for you and your household.

I knew a woman who lived alone in a rented two-bedroom house. Like me, she hated to wash dishes, which was apparent by the mess on the counters, in the sink, on the stove, and on the tables. However, she owned enough dishes to plate up an army. She had sets of dishes for every occasion, but she rarely had company. The walls were filled from bottom to top with dusty pictures, plaques, and other items. Every type of chair you can imagine filled the rooms, many piled with unfinished projects and laundry. The house, like the woman, was in a constant state of confusion. In my mind, she would have been better off, and happier, if she reduced her belongings down to the basics, i.e., two or three chairs, enough plates for herself and what company she did have on occasion, a table, a few well-chosen works of art for the walls, a bed, a dresser, and a few lamps. Instead of living in that constant state of confusion, frustrated all the time because she couldn't get to the house to clean it, she could eliminate things until she found it manageable.

I love going to garage sales and secondhand stores, but I live with one rule: whatever I choose to purchase, I must be willing to give something up, and I'm not talking about money. Since I like what I have, it keeps me from purchasing useless items. The other thing I do is question my motives. Will I use it? What will I use it for? Do I want to clean it? How much time and effort am I willing to give up for it? That's how I keep from cluttering my house with needless, useless stuff that I neither want to find a place for or clean.

Scrutinize your shopping feelings. Do you buy things because it makes you feel good, like a quick fix? How bad do you want the item? If you were forced to give up something you already have for it, would you? Are you going to actually use the item, or will it end up taking up the space you could have for something you know you would use? Questioning is the simple solution to overbuying.

I can't read your minds, but I bet some of you are saying to yourself, "But I'm a collector." Do you know the difference between collecting and hoarding? A collector enjoys seeing his or her collection; displaying it, touching it, and caring for it, not stashing it under the bed, in the top of a closet, or in the back of the garage. When a collection ends up in those places, it becomes nothing more than clutter.

There are some for whom clutter becomes an addiction. For them, it goes much deeper than the physical things; it goes back to the clutter of mind, emotions, and spirituality. If you find yourself in that position, I would tell you to seek help as if you were any other addict. There is an anonymous program for clutter addicts. See the end of this chapter for more information.

How you live can affect, and reflect, how you see yourself, others, and the world around you. When you live in clutter, and have turned your house into an abuser that keeps you unhappy, it will affect your feelings of self-worth. It will reflect back to you that you are not good enough because you can no longer manage the problem. It can bring on shame and guilt that may keep you from allowing others into your life for fear of harsh judgment.

The world will seem like a darker place if you feel as if others can do things of which you feel incapable, and if you wonder what others say about the way you live. Feelings of fear and isolation can ensue.

The solution begins with awareness of what you have, what you need, and what is clutter. The next step is to decide whether your house enhances the way you want to live or is an overwhelming burden that has a hold on you. Then, get into action. Make those changes you know need to be made to turn your house into a home. I use the word "house," but

Small Bites

When I take a huge bite of ice cream, I get a brain freeze. If I try to swallow a big bite of meat, I choke. I experience the same things when I attempt to take on life in big bites. In each phase of my life, there are new things to worry over, different types of relationships, and problems to be solved. When I try to solve today's problems based on the past, I choke. When I assume future problems, believe that I somehow know what's going to happen down the road, my brain freezes up with fear.

In my mid-teens, I got pregnant by an older man, who married me to keep from going to jail, then left. For years after that, whenever I went into an intimate relationship, it was with the idea of protecting my heart from the inevitable end. I lived with the constant fear of abandonment; watched for it, waited for it, held back a part of me to survive the end, and saw everything and everyone as a threat. The thoughts that lived in the back of my mind were: How will I survive? Where will I go? How will I care for my child? What's going to happen to us?

Because of my fear, based on a past experience, paranoia, and jealousy, I choked, and destroyed one relationship after another. That's not terribly surprising because I kept getting involved with men I didn't love so the pain wouldn't be so bad when the relationship was over. I stayed in some miserable, abusive relationships, jobs, and other situations in an absolute brain freeze caused by questions and fears about the future. My rationale was that where I was, whom I was with, or what I was doing might not be great, but what if I went out there and it was worse? Even though the situation wasn't good and I was unhappy, at least I knew what to expect.

Are you choking on past experiences, allowing them to influence the decisions you're making today? Are you living in a state of brain freeze, unhappy and unsatisfied with your life because of questions about the future, and fear? What do you use to rationalize what you're doing, or not doing, as the case may be?

You may think that if you stay in control you will be able to protect yourself from pain, but it is an illusion. What of the pain of regret you will know one day when you realize what you missed out on in your life? When I've spent time with those in their final stages of life, I see that they are no longer concerned about what they did in the past, and they know there is no future; therefore, they speak of what was left undone. Do you want to be one of those people who dies with the words, "I wish I would have . . ." on your lips?

You may think corny sayings like "one day at a time" are just some silly words people in recovery use, but they are so much more. It's about taking life in small bites. Since you have no idea when your last moment will be, when you awake in the morning, granted another day, you have a decision to make. What will you do with your day? If it's your last, will it have been enough?

I can tell a lot about people and their attitudes about their lives simply by listening to them talk. Those who are unhappy or dissatisfied with their lives speak of what happened yesterday and what is coming up tomorrow. Those who are living fully, with that wonderful zest for life, talk about today with a hint of enthusiasm, even excitement in their voice. What are you talking about? When you talk about today, is it colored by the past or geared toward the future?

When I began to understand and embrace the concept of living one day at a time, I realized the same principle could work in all facets of my life. If I took everything, whether it was work, relationships, situations, or problems, down to small bites, I could deal with them. When I wake up in the morning and approach my typewriter, I go there with the idea of writing one sentence. That's all I have to accomplish. If it leads to another, that's great, but if it doesn't, that's okay too. If I think of the entire manuscript, it becomes confusing and overwhelming. Just for that moment, I only do what I can do, and let it go.

Faced with a problem, I ask myself some questions. What can I do about it today? How much of the day am I willing to give up to worry over something out of my control? Many people who deal with serious illnesses and treatments understand the concept. I knew a man with incurable cancer. He gathered all the information he could about his condition and what treatments were available to him so that he could make an informed decision. He decided against the debilitating treatments that might, or might not, give him a bit more time. He lived nearly five years, and he lived each day in the solution, not the problem. You might think there was no solution because his disease was incurable, but you would be wrong. Instead of wasting what time he had left worried over when he would die, how he would die, he lived . . . really lived, just as he had before the illness.

Life is like an incurable disease we all have in common. Until something drastic in the world changes, we cannot avoid death. Unless we choose to opt out of this life on our own terms, there is no way of knowing how and when it will happen. I go back to my questions: What can I do about it today? How much of my day am I willing to give up to worry over something beyond my control?

If I encounter a financial situation, and know there is no way to pay the whole debt, what are my choices? I can tell myself that if I can't pay it completely, I won't pay any of it, spend the money elsewhere, and carry the burden throughout the day worrying about the consequences, or I can be honest with whomever I owe, pay what I can that day, and be able to let it go because I know I did the best I could with what I had at that moment.

In a relationship problem, I can look at my part in the problem, make amends if needed, and understand that the other person involved has a choice in how he or she acts or reacts. As long as I take responsibility and do everything I can to make it right, what the other person chooses to do is out of my control. It's a matter of respect. Can I walk away from the problem with self-respect? Can I respect the other person's choices that affect his or her life?

If you have chosen to believe in a God of your understanding, to make spirituality a part of your life, what do you do with that? Is it a part-time situation, acknowledged only when it is convenient, or does it travel with you throughout your day and influence how you live? What is the point of being spiritual, of having beliefs, if you don't apply them to every situation, each day of your life? Today, if a troubled friend came to you for support and compassion, you would most likely accommodate that person. What of the ragged, homeless man sitting outside the door of your business?

How would you feel about him? What would you do? You might be saying to yourself, "That's different." If part of your belief system is that you are compassionate to other human beings, what is the difference?

Each day is a brand-new experience, filled with opportunities. What if it is the ability to recognize the daily opportunities, no matter how small they might seem, and how we act on them, that is the most important part of our life here on earth? Can handing a hungry person a cup of coffee and a sandwich elevate your spirit to a level that closing that big million-dollar deal can't?

All you have to deal with today, is today. It's wonderful to have plans for the future as long as you don't give up this moment for those moments that may never come, and that you understand plans change and accept that the results may be beyond your control. You do not have to be perfect, but you should strive for progress through the awareness of the significance of each day as a lifetime.

The next time you sit down to dinner with a big steak in front of you, or stop and buy a double-dipped ice cream cone, remember how difficult and painful it would be to eat either one in huge bites, and apply that idea to your life. Cut your life, your problems, up into small, manageable bites, do the best you can with each situation or opportunity, each day, and let it go. All the worry in the world will not change a thing, except the quality of your life.

TIPS FOR KEEPING IT SIMPLE AND SANE

- You can use the AWE Factor as a tool to change what you don't like about your life by consistently practicing awareness, willingness, and effort.

- You get to where you want to be by redefining your life with a beginner's mindset. This requires openness, honesty, and willingness.

- Where you are spiritually will influence your attitude about your body. If you believe the body is all there is, it can become all-important. It's easier to keep things in perspective if you see the body simply as the shell you were given to carry your mind, heart, and soul through a lifetime.

- The secret to making any relationship work is to live separately together. Be exactly who you are no matter whom you are with, where you are, and what you are doing. You have a right to your passions and dreams as much as anyone else, and should allow the other person those same rights.

- You can't like yourself if you don't know and accept yourself; when you avoid communicating with yourself and getting to know who you are, you put yourself at risk for adopting self-destructive behavior.   →

- The symptoms of financial clutter are constant feelings of pressure and stress. The solution is clarity and living within your means.

- Improving your life requires a clean sweep of your mind; you need to unclutter your mental, emotional, physical, and spiritual issues.

- Keep the bites you take out of your problems small and manageable, and do what you can with them one day at a time. Let the things that are beyond your control go—the only thing that worry is going to change is the quality of your life.

Summary

For when the One Great Scorer comes to write against your name, He marks—not that you won or lost—but how you played the game.

—Grantland Rice

Free to Be

Throughout human history, there have been those brave souls who have taught us about freedom. They stood up, spoke out, and acted in ways that many times cost them their very lives. Physically they may be gone, but they live on in the hearts and minds of those who were affected by their struggles and courage. Can you imagine what it must have been like for them to have been willing to lay everything on the line for freedom?

Do you think these people were more than human? Did they know fear? Courage is not about being fearless, but walking through the fear. When the pain caused by a situation becomes greater than the fear, heroes and heroines are born.

Is there a hero or heroine in your life—someone whom you wish to emulate? What is it about that individual that you so admire? Or are you waiting to meet that person, sure that who they are, what they stand for, can change your life? That may seem an unusual thing to ask, but you might be surprised at those who are waiting for another person to show them the secret to a happier, more fulfilled life.

Although I didn't recognize them at the time because I couldn't see past my pain, a lot of heroes and heroines crossed my path. If I did happen to glimpse them in my peripheral vision and recognize them, I turned my head and hurried away. The last thing I wanted to be confronted with when I lived and thought the way I did was somebody who had been willing to do those things I was not willing to do.

This book is about becoming your own hero or heroine; throwing off the shackles of past resentments and regrets, future fears, and learning what it means to be "free to be." When the war inside, the pain, becomes bigger than the fear of change, you are ready to begin.

You begin by cleaning out the clutter by whatever means you choose. Know your enemy, even if it's one that lives within. Ferret out information by reading books, searching on the Internet, and through others who have suffered from the same problem. Open your mind to solutions. Make a decision. Get into action.

Action begins by doing one thing differently in one moment. To replace an old habit, you must train yourself to take on a new habit. For years, I suffered from obsessive-compulsive disorder, or OCD. Compulsion is an irresistible impulse to perform an irrational act. Although my problem was not as severe as many others, it was affecting my life in a negative way, and certainly fed into my addictions.

My OCD began early in life and got continually worse as the years went by. No matter how poorly I lived or how bad my residence was, everything had to be spotless and in its place. I couldn't go to bed, leave the house, or allow anyone else into my living space unless it was perfect. I don't mean I didn't want to do those things, but that I had lost the choice. I couldn't function otherwise.

Do you know why? I didn't, until a therapist friend of mine told me. He said that the more cluttered and disorganized my thoughts and feelings became, the harder I tried to control my surroundings in the vain hope and illusion that somehow my perfect surroundings would help me control my out of whack thoughts and emotions. When it didn't work, even though I continued to do it, I fell into addictions to escape.

He also pointed out that I was going about the solution backwards. If I really wanted a solution, to free myself from my obsessive-compulsive behavior, it would be necessary for me to go to the root of the problem: my cluttered mind and feelings. When that happened, my behavior would manifest itself outside of me. He was right. Every step I took forward to balance my mental and emotional chaos lessened the need to control my surroundings and the need to escape.

Today, cleaning can be good therapy for me, but I know the *need* to clean is not. Life is messy, and I can choose to spend mine cleaning it or living it. The main thing is that

I have a choice, and the knowledge that I have a choice is what has set me free.

What are those things that hold you prisoner? How are they affecting your life? Can you put a name to them? Are you willing to become informed, or fear that if you say them out loud, and figure out a solution, that you might actually have to take action? That is the fear you must walk through to discover what it is to be free, to have a choice. That is how you become your own hero or heroine. The life you save will be your own.

Remember the exhilaration you felt when you experienced those first moments of freedom: the first time you drove a car alone, or shared an adult kiss, or went on a trip without a chaperone, or any of the other first tastes of freedom in your life? You can experience that same feeling as you clear out the clutter of mind, body, and spirit.

As I'm writing this, I'm picturing the character Scrooge in the movie *A Christmas Carol*, jumping up and down on his bed when he realizes he's been given another chance in life, that he has a choice, and can choose to do things differently. He went from being a stingy, selfish, hateful, miserable person to a kind, giving, loving individual because of his dead friend who carried his burdens in the form of great chains and weights and the ghosts who presented him the truth. The change began with his realization of the way he thought and felt, and how it had affected his actions. The exhilaration shown as he leaps up and down on the bed, kisses the housekeeper, buys the goose, and shocks others because of his drastic change, was brought on because he was finally free to be.

Yes, he was just a fictional character that lived in a book and a movie. However, Scrooge, and the *Christmas Carol* story line have lived with us for decades, and the concept has been copied over and over. The reason for that is that so many of us can either relate to Scrooge or one of the characters affected by Scrooge in the story.

If you were to write a movie script in which you played the Scrooge character, what events would take place to cause you to change? What of those you've known, who've crossed over? What would they tell you about the links in their chains, and what they represent? What would the ghosts of past, present, and future teach you about your life and where you're headed?

If you had a chance to change things, what would you do differently? The good news is that you are not a fictional character, and as long as you are drawing breath in this life, there is an opportunity for change; there is hope.

I began the change by examining one negative thought at a time. When a person did something I didn't like, and a negative thought entered my mind, I told myself. "This is not about me, and it's none of my business. He (or she) has to live with his own choices." As I practiced rethinking, it became a new habit. Each time a negative emotion flared, I examined it. What was it really about? It was usually about a lack of control over people, places, and things. Each time I could successfully accept the true reason about a feeling and why I had it, it became easier on the next occasion. My actions changed as a result of training myself to rethink and taking responsibility for my own feelings.

The change didn't happen overnight, like it did for Scrooge, but it did happen. I didn't have to die to carry the chains of regret around with me. They were there, forged by me; my self-pity, rage, resentment, regrets, and actions. With each link I dropped off, I knew a small taste of freedom from bondage, until one day I realized I'd gone through a whole day without a negative thought, a bad feeling, or doing anything destructive. I was happy, because I was finally free to be.

What does "free to be" mean? For me, it means living in the moment, exactly as I am, doing the best that I can do, and always striving forward. It means accepting that I am not perfect, I will never be perfect, but I don't have to be. It's about leaving other people, and a God of my understanding, to their business and taking care of mine. It is not my job to change the world or anyone in it, but to live in the truth of who I am, do what I can, where and when I can, and leave the rest to a power greater than I.

I may not go down in history as a great person who taught the world about freedom, but if I can leave this world knowing I gave the best I had in me to myself and others, it will be enough. If I have known happiness, peace, and what it is to be free to be, it is more than I ever dreamed. I laid everything that I was on the line, became willing to live in the truth, made the choice to stand up, speak up, and act accordingly, and have never looked back, or known regret. I am free to be.

Life Is Not a Spectator Sport

In the game of life, you are either a player or a spectator. It's that simple. If you see yourself as a player, the big question is, how are you playing the game? If you are sitting on the sidelines, the questions are why, and do you want to get into the game?

A player is one who is willing to take the risk, who gives everything he or she has to the game, and who understands it's not about winning or losing, but being involved in the game. The player knows that there will be heartache and joy, errors and crowning moments, and everything in between, and that all those things are an essential part of the game.

Those who excel at the game are the ones who practice every day, review their playbacks, pay attention to errors, and adjust accordingly. They learn through their mistakes and try not to repeat the performance. When they can't figure things out, they ask for help from others who know more about the game.

If you had to review a playback at the end of each day of your life, what would you see? Would you be satisfied with how you performed? Would you be willing to see errors on your part, or would you blame others for your mistakes? When life is going well, and you are experiencing one of those crowning moments, do you set yourself above the other players and think you are doing it all on your own? Do you continue to practice, or do you think you've arrived, and are no longer required to do those things it takes to progress?

You don't have to die not to live. I know that from personal experience. Before I got in the game of life, I ran around pretending to be a player, trying in every way I could to convince everyone that I was a player, but just because I was moving fast and doing stuff didn't mean I was involved in life. It was a lie that I lived out on a daily basis. I might as well have been glued to a seat in the nosebleed section. The glue that held me fast as nothing more than a spectator was fear.

I believed God and everyone else existed for one sole purpose—to make my life miserable. How self-important was I? I was sitting in the stands expecting life to be delivered to me like a hot dog. When I didn't get it when and the way I wanted it, I experienced rage. Needless to say, I was angry most of the time. It never occurred to me to stand up, go after what I wanted, and fix it the way I wanted it. It was easier to stay where I was, and complain about everyone else and how they'd mistreated me.

I could lie to everyone else, but somewhere in the deepest part of me lived the truth. Because of that, my mind was cluttered with conflicting thoughts. I wanted to jump out of the stands, be a part of life, and experience all those wonderful highs. I wanted to be a winner. Fear of not being good enough, rejection, and pain through loss, warred with those thoughts, and won. Therefore, the only highs I knew for years were manufactured through chemicals. Believe me when I tell you that it's not the same thing.

What kind of thought war goes on in your mind? Which thoughts are winning? How are they affecting your life? If you think your thoughts do not affect your feelings, you would be wrong. Remember the hot dog? I told myself that was what brought on my rage, but it was simply easier to blame something outside myself than to admit I was angry with myself because I didn't have the guts to do what was needed to get what I wanted.

If you've decided that you are a spectator, and have chosen to remain in the stands at a safe distance from life, personally unaffected by the outcome, you need to know that there isn't enough distance to keep you safe and unaffected by life. A pigeon might poop on your head. It could rain. The stands could collapse. You could be hit in the head by a foul ball, or fall down and get trampled by overexcited fans. In life, no matter where you are or what you're doing, no matter how safe you think you are, things happen, and you will feel the effects.

When that epiphany hit me, I discovered a great secret that had eluded me for the first half of my life: there is no such thing as a spectator in life. If you're here, you are a part of the game, whether you want to be or not. The truth was that I was a player; I just wasn't a very good one. You are a player. How are you playing the game of life?

We each have a position to play on the human team. If we want a new position, we must retrain ourselves, practice, and be willing to do whatever it takes to achieve our goal. That willingness may include putting aside fear and false pride, and asking for help, whether human, spiritual, or both. Some may see asking for help as a sign of weakness. I see it as what a strong player does. After all, if you were trying to improve your golf game, there would be no shame in getting an instructor.

The purpose of this book is to help you become aware that if you are not happy with the position you occupy in life, you have a choice. I have shared with you some of the things that helped me clear away the clutter of my life and work toward changing my position, in the hope that it might inspire you to do the same. If you are unhappy and discontent, don't settle by convincing yourself you don't deserve more. Strive for those crowning moments, and know that success isn't simply about that one moment, but the striving forward as well. The game of life is simple if you don't complicate it.

TIPS FOR KEEPING IT SIMPLE AND SANE

- "Free to be" means living in the truth of who you are, doing what you can in the moment, and trusting everything else to a God of your understanding.

- There is no such thing as a spectator in life; if you're here, then you are part of the game, whether you like it or not. You might as well get into the game, because there is no distance you can go where it won't affect you in some way.

The Twelve Steps

1. We admitted we were powerless—that our lives had become unmanageable.

2. Came to believe that a Power greater than ourselves could restore us to sanity.

3. Made a decision to turn our will and our lives over to the care of God as we understood Him.

4. Made a searching and fearless moral inventory of ourselves.

5. Admitted to God, to ourselves, and to another human being the exact nature of our wrongs.

6. Were entirely ready to have God remove all these defects of character.

7. Humbly asked Him to remove our shortcomings.

8. Made a list of all persons we had harmed, and became willing to make amends to them all.

9. Made direct amends to such people wherever possible, except when to do so would injure them or others.

10. Continued to take personal inventory and when we were wrong promptly admitted it.

11. Sought through prayer and meditation to improve our conscious contact with God, as we understood Him, praying only for knowledge of His will for us and the power to carry that out.

12. Having had a spiritual awakening as the result of these Steps, we tried to carry this message to addicts, and to practice these principles in all our affairs.

About the Author

Barb Rogers learned most of her life lessons through great pain and tragedy. After surviving abuse, the death of her children, addiction, and life-threatening illness, she succeeded in finding a new way of life. She became a professional costume designer and founded Broadway Bazaar Costumes. When an illness forced her to give up costume designing, Barb turned to writing. She is the author of three costuming books and several titles on recovery, alcoholism and addiction, and well-being, including: *Twenty-Five Words, Clutter-Junkie No More,* and the Just Try This series. Barb lives in Arizona with her husband and their two dogs.

To Our Readers

Conari Press, an imprint of Red Wheel/Weiser, publishes books on topics ranging from spirituality, personal growth, and relationships to women's issues, parenting, and social issues. Our mission is to publish quality books that will make a difference in people's lives—how we feel about ourselves and how we relate to one another. We value integrity, compassion, and receptivity, both in the books we publish and in the way we do business.

Our readers are our most important resource, and we value your input, suggestions, and ideas about what you would like to see published. Please feel free to contact us, to request our latest book catalog, or to be added to our mailing list.

Conari Press
An imprint of Red Wheel/Weiser, LLC
500 Third Street, Suite 230
San Francisco, CA 94107
www.redwheelweiser.com